THE LEADERSHIP TOOLBOX

14 Strategies that Build a CHAIN REACTION OF SUCCESS

VICKI BRACKETT

First published by Dog Ear Publishing
4011 Vincennes Road
Indianapolis, IN 46268
www.dogearpublishing.net

ISBN: 978-145756-760-5

This book is printed on acid-free paper.
Printed in the United States of America

Here's What People Are Saying

"Vicki's strengths are her leadership, strong customer focus and ability to get things done. She was instrumental in developing up and coming leaders. Her commitment to client satisfaction was superb and regular client feedback was testimony to her efforts to earn their satisfaction and loyalty." - R.F., President

"Vicki has had an immediate and significant impact on our business unit. Vicki is a strategic problem solver who is adept at working with front line staff and institutional leaders. As a result, her call-center management experience helped us adapt our processes, increasing contact rate." - F.C., COO

"Vicki was able to help us redefine our overall sales process by looking at the whole process, not just one part of it. The result was a significant increase in reach rate with a downstream conversion rate and revenue improvement. I would recommend Vicki to any organization that feels they could stand to improve their performance." - A.L., VP

"Vicki approached every day with fresh ideas that created enthusiasm and confidence among the sales team. We quickly developed processes and communication flows that improved our level of customer service and maximized the effective use of our resources. Vicki had a tremendous impact on our staff and we realized very positive results in a short period of time. Her guidance and leadership gave us the direction we needed to be successful and a competitive advantage in the marketplace.

"Vicki understands where the communication disconnects are, and has great suggestions for re-connection. She was an excellent coach to both new and old managers, and has the ability to assess organizational flaws with terrific insight. She brings with her a massive amount of tips and tricks, along with enthusiasm and positivity that is simply contagious." - B.L., Assistant Director

"Vicki is able to identify and capitalize on the strengths of individuals to build strong, well-rounded leadership teams. So with Vicki's mentoring, these leadership teams are able to achieve great success in a very short period of time." - J.L, Manager

"This would have exploded if I had not had the opportunity to get Vicki to step in and turn the site around. Her knowledge of business and people turned a site from complete failure into a success and delivering some star metrics. As a result, I believe that anyone that gets the opportunity to have Vicki work on a project will see tremendous results and learn more than ever expected." - F.M., Senior Global Vendor Manager

"Vicki has had an immediate and significant impact on our enrollment unit. Vicki is a strategic problem solver who is adept at working with front line staff and institutional leaders. As a result, her call center management experience helped us adapt our processes, increasing contact rates and ultimately new student registrations." - B.B., COO

"Vicki's ability to mentor is surpassed only by her genuine desire to see others succeed. She gave sound advice and did not hold back on what needed improvement. I count the time spent with Vicki equal to a master's degree in management." - J.F., Director

"Vicki has a special gift when it comes to empowering others and has the skill set and confidence needed to accomplish what seems un-accomplishable. So, any company lucky enough to gain her as part of their leadership team will discover just how rare of a gem that she truly is." - C.L., VP

Disclaimer

The stories and case studies that appear in this book come from the author's personal career experiences. The names of individuals, companies, and other identifying facts have been changed to protect the identities. Therefore, any identifying resemblance to actual individuals is merely coincidental.

THE LEADERSHIP TOOLBOX

TOOLBOX

14 Strategies that Build a
Chain Reaction of Success

VICKI BRACKETT

Contents

Acknowledgement

I remember my first big holiday ramp when my Fortune 500 client asked me to double the number of customer service representatives in my business unit, while keeping our excellent customer service performance consistent. With brand new customer service representatives, newly promoted leadership with no previous management experience, and processes that had never been tested within an organization of that size, the client's request felt overwhelming.

There are three things that always come to mind when I am about to tackle a challenge. First, I hear my Dad telling me to "fake it 'til you make it" and "never let them see you sweat." Second, I remember that a great leader harnesses the talents of the people to make great things happen. Lastly, I remind myself that failure is never an option. These three philosophies have become part of my belief system. I have lived by them throughout my entire career, as I led organizations of 50 to over 2,000 employees in start-up, small, midsize, and Fortune 500 companies. I realize that with the right people and strategies, an organization can accomplish great things, exceeding employee, client and customer expectations.

Through the years, many of the CEOs and presidents I worked with, along with employees I led, asked me to write a book about my strategic approach to turning operations around, building world class teams, and doing the "impossible." For years, the task of writing a book that would systematically take the reader through my leadership tools seemed as overwhelming as that first holiday ramp. At first, I felt that I was too busy raising my family and working. Then, after my two children were raised and out of the house on their own, I told myself that my life and work were just too busy to attempt this project. Thankfully, I eventually ran out of excuses. I decided to utilize the three philosophies of my belief system and tackle this project.

The process of writing *The Leadership Toolbox* was difficult at times, especially finding time to write. I knew that failure was not an option though, so I committed myself to the project and pushed myself to create a book that will provide value to the reader. The editing process also proved challenging. After working with one editor for six months, I realized that I had made an error in my hiring decision. I ended the agreement and found myself interviewing individuals for a second time. I wanted an editor who not only had the right skill sets, but also exemplified passion and a strong work ethic. I needed someone that would put their ego on the back burner, so they could listen to my voice and help me articulate my systematic approach to *The Leadership Toolbox*. A trusted colleague recommended Erika Winston.

Erika took painstaking efforts to talk with me about the "whys" and the "hows" of what I had accomplished in moving organizations through various challenges, with different levels of skill sets and professional maturity – all quicker than executive teams thought possible. She helped me lay out each tool of *The Leadership Toolbox* in a simple to understand format, illustrated by case studies and stories. I am forever grateful to Erika for taking a personal stake in the success of my goal, going above and beyond the call of duty to get this book completed and ready for publishing.

Second, I would like to thank the special colleagues and friends who have read chapters, offered their expertise and opinions, and cheered me on to completion of my book:

Diana Page Jordan, Shauna Whidden, Diane Epstein, Suzan Steinberg, Velma Kirksey-Tarver, Pamela Gardner, Lyndsay Jane DeVore, Dryden Annie Keaton, Ji Ju, Louise Le Gat, Corine Wofford, Deborah Beckman Horton, Bryan Blume, Aaron Billings, Jody Schmidt, Kelly Morgan, Deb Beroset, Cynthia Carrese, Dan Carrese, Catrice Monson, Nick Bryditzki and Micheline Green. Thanks to Kim Carpenter, Jane Deuber, Barbarah Nicoll, Deb Boulanger, Morna Haist, Ronda Renee, Sarah Michael, Monique Mayers, Alisoun Mackenzie, Kristen Watts, and Nicola Lytle for their input.

Special thanks to Daphne Parsekian for additional editing. Her attention to detail and level of service contributed to the success of this project. There are so many others who have been supportive throughout this process, and I appreciate each of these special individuals.

I was so fortunate to have my "sister" Deni Maher's tireless commitment to keep my feet to the fire, so I could honor my true purpose in writing this book. She supported me throughout the entire process, including helping to connect me with Adriano, who designed the book cover. Thank you to my brother, Nicholas, for his creative expertise and support.

Acknowledgement and a heartfelt thank you to Art Bergen for his love, support, and willingness to set aside our personal time together, so I could have additional time to write. He made sure that we had several wonderful vacations and four-day weekends during this process so that I could rest, relax, and clear my head.

No mother could have more support than I have had. I would like to thank my two children, Josh and Julie, for standing beside me through life's challenges and triumphs as well as lovingly supporting me as I wrote this book. You provided me with tireless support during every step of this process. Thank you for helping me brainstorm, and reading chapters throughout this endeavor.

Lastly, I would like to acknowledge and thank the thousands of employees, CEOs, executive and management teams that helped me vet the tools in *The Leadership Toolbox* through the years. The successes that *we* have accomplished have been many. It's been fun and rewarding, as we have served each other, while assisting our customers and clients across the globe.

My intent in writing this book is to help leaders, at all levels, with a systematic and methodical approach to building a chain reaction of success in their organization – while having fun. As the achievement of my first big holiday launch exemplified, there is nothing like success to fuel the flames of passion as we go to work every day. I have seen the effect the tools in *The Leadership Toolbox* can have on an organization and now they are available to leaders everywhere. Thanks to everyone who helped to make this happen.

I dedicate this book to my children, Josh and Julie.

I cherish the relationship I have with both of you.

How to Get the Best Return on Investment by Reading This Book

It was my first day of work as the Director of Operations for a contact center outsourcing company. I had been working about three hours when the CEO walked into my office and made a request that sent my head swirling. "Vicki, I am not going to be able to make payroll this week. I am wondering if you will hold onto your first paycheck and not cash it for about a week." I looked at him in disbelief. Less than three hours on the job and this was the first request coming from the executive team? What had I missed? Did I not ask the right questions during the interview process?

This was not a tiny operation. In fact, they had been in business for over 10 years. Their operations consisted of a large fulfillment center, the contact center, and a large client services organization serving almost 100 clients in the business-to-consumer and business-to-business industry verticals. It was not a company where payroll should be an issue. My head continued to swirl as I stared at the CEO. He must have sensed that I was having trouble getting my mind around this conversation because he quickly tried to explain. "I really need your help. We are struggling a lot. Everything I own is wrapped up in my business. If anyone can move my company forward and out of this hole, I think you can."

My thoughts quickly turned to my two children (whom I was raising as a single mother), my mortgage, my bills, and the fact that I needed to earn a living and support my family. Yet, in the back of my mind, I could hear the familiar voice of my dad telling me to "fake it until you make it." A business leader himself, my dad's words of wisdom had never steered me wrong before and I decided to follow them in that moment. Even though I needed that first paycheck, I looked at the CEO and said, "Not a problem. We can talk about it later. Let's get this business turned around." His face filled with relief as he thanked me for taking this new role and walked out of my office.

That incident was a tipping point in my career. It was the catalyst that caused me to consciously look at and use leadership tools that I had been developing and cultivating since my early 20s. Two decades later, *The Leadership Toolbox* emerged as a proven systematic process for helping employees and business leaders quickly implement solutions that impact their revenue and bottom line in 90 to 120 days. These very practical approaches have consistently resulted in quantifiable outcomes for organizations, and in much shorter periods of time than the executives that hired me thought possible. My clients have seen first-hand the real and impactful results that are possible with the tools. Entire company cultures have been turned around or enhanced quickly and efficiently. After years of utilizing these tools in organizations, both in groups and in one-on-one interactions, many executives and employees encouraged me to write them down. I finally took their advice and *The Leadership Toolbox* was born.

I designed these tools to be a practical and systematic approach to leadership, purposely tailoring them for easy implementation within virtually any organization – from small start-ups to Fortune 100 multinational companies. Though I have been in the sales, technical support, e-commerce, and customer service contact center environments for 20 years of my career, these tools can be effectively utilized in any vertical or industry.

Some of my clients have been surprised that strategies so simple can bring about such powerful results, but the power of these tools actually lies in their simplicity. They are foolproof and easy to understand. Employee and leadership confidence is built by practicing the tools in real work situations and seeing the results (almost immediately in some cases). Multiply that confidence by every employee in your company and that's when you really experience the chain reaction effect of *The Leadership Toolbox*. Things start moving forward rapidly. Other employees begin duplicating leaders' efforts, which provides them with greater knowledge of what it takes to be a leader. Through this process, two key benefits emerge. First, when they move into leadership positions, they already know how to perform the duties, so there is less of a learning curve. Secondly, it creates excitement within the organization, which is why the results are so quick and phenomenal.

Who Can Benefit From This Approach to Leadership?

With a practical and systematic framework in mind, I am writing this book for two distinct audiences. The first are leaders within organizations who struggle with how to properly motivate and manage front-line employees who are levels down in the organization. They know these front-line employees hold the keys to unlock real, sustained financial success and rely on other managers to drive that growth. In many instances, these companies engage expensive training programs and consultants, only to find that the new techniques don't stick and provide little traction to significantly drive performance.

Most people are promoted within an organization because people like them, and they performed well at their previous position. However, without proper mentoring and the cultivation of leadership skills, these new leaders may have no vision or understanding of how to position the organization for growth. They may satisfactorily manage tasks and projects, but they are doing nothing to actively drive greater results from their teams. How do we encourage these new leaders to motivate, lead, and mentor the future leaders of the organization? How do we inspire them to drive organizational growth, so they can continue moving up the ladder? With *The Leadership Toolbox*, your leaders will develop deeper leadership skill sets and be ready to move up within the organization quicker.

The second audience is the Human Resources organization. These are individuals who are tasked with identifying appropriate training and increasing employee engagement and retention, while enhancing diversity and inclusion. They can face significant challenges with the operations side of the organization, particularly when trying to find programs that can engage employees and impact organizational metrics. *The Leadership Toolbox* creates an authentically inclusive environment that organically engages employees.

One of my core beliefs is that we can systematically and proactively affect our key performance indicators – whether focused on top line revenue or bottom line profit – before we see those numbers trending in the wrong direction. To accomplish this goal, we need an approach that is easy, fun, and engaging for all employees. When employees are engaged naturally, you will see positive traction and have long-term success.

What Kind of Results Can You Experience?

Whether you are looking to increase productivity, safety scores, sales revenue, customer service satisfaction scores, net promotor scores, client satisfaction, or employee engagement, *The Leadership Toolbox* can help your organization reach its goal. If your focus is on recurring issues of employee absenteeism and attrition, these tools have resulted in immediate and drastic effects for companies.

Examples of some of the success that have been accomplished within organizations include:

- Employee attrition reduced from 90% annually to 10% annually in just 90 days.
- Employee absenteeism reduced by 50% in 90 days.
- Customer Service Satisfaction Scores increased from 59% to 90% in five months.
- Client bases salvaged and grown within four months – doubling gross revenue.
- Sales conversion increased by 200%.
- Drastically reduced employee attrition from 400% annualized to below industry averages.
- Savings of millions of dollars in recruiting and training costs.

Each of the tools in *The Leadership Toolbox* has been vetted by thousands of employees and dozens of organizations over the course of 20 years. Each tool includes suggestions for real world usage and one or more case studies illustrating how the tools can be utilized to address specific types of challenges. The case studies also exemplify how to use the tools as building blocks to achieve desired results.

The tools in *The Leadership Toolbox* will show you how to:

- Duplicate a manager's efforts so that results are achieved faster, without additional labor costs.

- Build creative team structures that engage employees and increase skill sets, while quickly driving projects and KPIs.

- Develop authentic inclusion that engages employees and creates an environment where they want to come to work and perform.

- Instill the right behaviors in an employee or leader without telling them what to do or how to act.

- Achieve exemplary customer satisfaction scores and sales conversion rates with lower training costs.

- Infuse a leadership mindset in your front-line employees so you can move towards your goals faster and build a deeper leadership bench, so you are ready for growth.

- Engage front-line employees so they don't hinder new initiatives and drag down your progress.

- Train a second and/or third-level leader to manage through other leadership levels.

- Close process gaps quickly without employees and managers engaging in a tug of war.

- Build collaboration with departments that historically have huge egos and don't like to be questioned.

- Increase your leadership bench more quickly, with minimal costs, so leaders are ready to be successful when they are promoted to the next level.

- Understand when someone is really ready to promote, so you don't regret your decision later.

- Build top-producing teams despite fluctuations in the economy.

- Retain the right talent to drive business and increase revenue/net profit.

- Develop innovative employee engagement programs that drive bottom line results.

Throughout my career, I have been passionate about developing a systematic approach to leading people that is simple, practical, and easy to replicate. There is a way to not only survive, but stay competitive in today's business landscape.

The Leadership Toolbox has changed the way I navigate through my day. Unlike most senior leaders, I engage with more employees, customers and clients. The CEOs I report to have been shocked at what their teams can achieve so quickly. I believe in *The Leadership Toolbox* and stake my reputation on these proven tools. I invite you to learn and utilize them within your organization. Are you ready to get started? If so, here are some of my tips for getting the most out of this book.

Getting Started

I was having a series of strategic discussions with a multibillion-dollar multinational company that was struggling with building a consistently performing, work from home contact center organization. The marketing department had done a great job building the company brand in the market place and the organization had won many awards in the industry. However, when you "looked under the sheets," this organization was struggling with low employee engagement scores, high employee absenteeism, high employee attrition, and customer service scores that continually hovered at just average across all enterprises. They were looking for someone who had a proven track record in building rock solid, top-performing virtual/work from home environments, which could be scaled quickly for product launches and seasonal surges in customer interaction.

I set up a call with the Senior Director of Global Operations. From the information I gathered, I went into the conversation believing this director would be a linear thinker, data driven, and extremely process driven. I was careful during my discussion to articulate my talking points with stories that included specific data points. After each story, I drew a logical conclusion and gave him additional data points. I made sure each narrative included the actions that I took to gain those results. However, even after my lengthy explanation, he asked, "*How* did you accomplish all of this?"

I provided follow up answers, with additional information and data points. But I could tell that he still wasn't getting the information he wanted.

Next, he asked me to give him the chronological order of exactly what I did to increase customer service satisfaction scores (CSATs) and achieve lower employee attrition at the same time. I gave him a more detailed explanation and backed it up with specific examples of how struggling front-line employees could achieve 90% CSATs in a virtual/work at home environment so quickly. I also tied that same process to an achievement where I had increased employee engagement that drove employee attrition down by 50% in a short period of time. As he continued asking questions, I suddenly realized that — in his mind — he had followed the same processes with no results. That's why he kept digging for additional answers.

Nearing the end of our scheduled conference time, he impatiently said, "I need to know *more* details." I wasn't getting anywhere, and I was at a loss as to what to say next. In hindsight, perhaps I should have told him it was magic.

Finally, I told him about *The Leadership Toolbox*. "They are tools and strategies that work. They are easy to teach and people at all levels, including front-line employees, love them." He asked me to explain one of the tools and I thought, "Heck, why not?"

So, I gave him the name of a tool in *The Leadership Toolbox* and explained how to use it in less than 30 seconds. I could almost hear his brain thinking through the phone, as he cynically commented, "That's going to get my employee attrition cut in half and increase CSATs?"

My answer to him was yes because *The Leadership Toolbox* differs from standard industry training programs. Some processes are so complicated that they fail to impact the organization. Employees find some training overwhelming and time-consuming, so they never fully learn how to implement it. *The Leadership Toolbox* is composed of simple strategies that can be utilized alone or as building blocks with other tools in the toolbox. They are designed to have dramatic effects on the culture by engaging, supporting, and cultivating the skill set of front-line employees and leaders. That's why progress is seen so quickly.

First Principle – Don't Let the Simplicity of the Tools Fool You

These tools are simple to understand and use, but the phenomenal results come from how you implement them.

Second Principle – Practice a Tool for 30 Days

The tools in *The Leadership Toolbox* allow employees and leaders alike to feel powerful and part of the solution. When employees feel good, they perform better. Use the tools every day. They can be utilized with each person you talk with, whether it be in person, on the phone, by chat, email, text, or on social media. They say 21 days create a habit. I say give it 30 days. After 30 days, you will own the tools in *The Leadership Toolbox* and see the results. It can happen that fast!

Third Principle – Measurable Results

An international consulting company reached out to me because of my expertise in working with organizations that are struggling. Their client, the largest manufacturer in an industry vertical, was struggling with low customer service satisfaction scores (CSATs) and low first touch resolution. The management team mostly consisted of family and friends who lacked the necessary skill sets to navigate through these challenges or grow the company.

As I talked with the CEO of the consulting company, she asked me specifically what deliverables her client could expect from my assistance. I paused for a moment and said, "Higher CSATs and higher first touch resolution." She expressed her surprise at my results-driven approach.

"What were you expecting?" I jokingly responded. She said that most consultants do the analysis and put their recommendations together, along with a list of activities they would agree to perform. However, they provide no promises for moving key performance indicators. "Well, analysis and a strategic, tactical game plan are important," I stated. "But if we work together, I will help your client's team put together a plan that gets them the results they are looking for. I know that certain activities drive performance, but if that doesn't result in positive change in the key performance indicators they are struggling with, then what good is it to pay for my services?" I quickly added, "They just don't know what to do to change their results. I can work with them in the trenches to figure that all out and, at the same time, infuse team members with new leadership skills. After all, if they knew what to do, wouldn't they already be doing it?"

When you utilize *The Leadership Toolbox*, your results should be measurable. Carefully review your key performance indicators after using the tools for 30 days. Some examples of common performance markers include sales units sold, sales revenue, sales conversion, first call resolution, customer service satisfaction scores, employee attrition, and employee absenteeism. Other possible results could be number of production days, days without an accident, or even the number of receivables that are less than 30 days. Every organization has specific key performance indicators that they drive. Effective implementation of the tools should bring about measurable results – it's that simple. Celebrate every success with your leaders and employees at all levels. Positive results will build enthusiasm and fuel the desire to become better leaders.

Fourth Principle – The Tools Are Designed as Building Blocks

The tools within *The Leadership Toolbox* are designed to be utilized independently or in combination with others. There are no rules on how or when to use them. As you read the case studies, you will discover that many of my employees and clients have used various tools simultaneously, with one building upon another, to more quickly meet their desired results. You can follow these examples exactly or use them as general guidelines for figuring out the best combination of tools within your organization. Don't worry about getting the tools in the right order. Just by practicing the individual tools, you will figure out where to use them in your conversations, emails, chats, and social media exchanges.

Fifth Principle – The Tools Proactively Engage Employees

A recent State of the American Workplace Report found out that only 33% of employees in the United States were engaged. That means that two out of three employees are not engaged and passionately contributing to the success of their companies. The report stated that these disengaged employees cost U.S. companies somewhere between $450 and $550 billion each year! That's a staggering amount of money that can and should be reduced.

The tools in *The Leadership Toolbox* create a culture that truly engages employees and helps them learn new skill sets while having fun. This systematic approach empowers each employee to notice gaps in processes and initiatives, and help their teams move through obstacles *before* the metrics start sliding backwards. As managers learn these concepts, they will have a variety of strategies to implement in order to move the organization forward.

When *The Leadership Toolbox* is utilized with front-line employees who want to be considered for promotion, you can cultivate leaders at the heart of your organization. Now, these leaders of tomorrow can help support their team or department today. This helps them feel a part of the leadership of their team. It allows future leaders to contribute and grow their own skill sets, which also increases their emotional and professional maturity. In organizations that suffer from high employee absenteeism and attrition, you can see these metrics dramatically decreased.

When you provide front-line employees with these new tools, they feel they have a stake in the success of the team or organization. In addition, the current leader has more time to mentor their own replacement, so they can move to the next level. In other words, your leadership bench can deepen quickly. When this is done across the entire organization, you will be able to get new leaders "on the bench," at every level, much more efficiently. This will energize your people and get them moving forward. They will have a stake in the success of the organization and move toward better performance results.

Keep these principles in mind as you read through the book and begin putting the tools into practice. I have used *The Leadership Toolbox* to successfully address countless challenges within dozens of companies. The impact is undeniable, and I am confident that these tools can help your organization build a chain reaction of success.

Make Money, Save Money, Mitigate Risk
Develop a Strategy That Everyone Can Get Behind

The town hall meeting was packed with more than 300 customer support center employees. Danny, a front-line agent, raised his hand and I called on him. He stood up and blurted out, "All this company cares about is making money! I hate companies like this!" Silence fell on the entire room. Everyone's eyes darted between Danny and me as they wondered what I was going to say. You could hear a pin drop.

I took a deep breath, looked Danny straight in the eye and said, "Thank you for speaking up and saying what a lot of people might be thinking. You mentioned to me yesterday that you wanted to be a leader, so I am not only going to address your comments, but also offer you some insight on how a leader might think about this situation. How does that sound?"

He looked at me with confusion and asked, "You are not mad at me for speaking up and saying how I feel about the company?"

"Absolutely not," I replied. "Because you are right. The company cares about making money." I turned my attention to the more than 300 employees assembled in the room and asked, "How many of you want to move into management at some point in your career?" Hands went up all over the room. "How many managers in the room have a goal to move into a position with more responsibility and compensation in the future?" All of the managers' hands went up. I went on, "Yes, Danny is right. The company cares about making money. Let's look at why."

1

I was brand new to the organization. Our client, a Fortune 500 consumer products company, had threatened to close this customer contact center due to unsatisfactory performance. I was told I was their "last hope" to turn operations around and keep their contract. There were 16 contact centers supporting this client, and in order to remain one of them, the organization had to ascend to "the middle of the pack" on customer service satisfaction scores (CSATs). At that time, they were sitting at number 14. I had one month to improve their performance, or the client was going to close our customer contact center down, resulting in over 300 agents, management, and support staff losing their jobs.

I spent the remainder of the town hall meeting explaining and discussing part one of the first tool in *The Leadership Toolbox*. I illustrated several case studies that showcased the concept and, by the time I finished, the employees not only understood the tool and the game plan, but even appeared enthusiastic about turning things around. Our customer service satisfaction scores soared from number 14 out of 16 international contact centers to number one in only three and a half weeks!

The Three Parts of Tool #1

Make the company money: Sometimes employees don't think about the *"why"* behind the company making money, and it's the responsibility of leaders to explain the *"why"* to them. The bottom line is that if there is no money, there is no company. It's that simple.

Save the company money: This can happen a few ways. For most leaders, it's about increasing productivity and minimizing expenses. It may also result from decreased tax liabilities or by moving money to other divisions or countries where the landscape is more business friendly. Part of leadership responsibility is thinking of ways to save the company money.

Mitigating risk: New leaders and most employees fail to consider risk during their work day. Mitigating risk takes into consideration what we say; how we interact with employees, clients, and customers; and how our processes are driven. As leaders, we have an obligation to mitigate risk that could put the company brand, financial strength, or legal position in jeopardy.

Leaders at every level need to understand the duty to "Make Money, Save Money, and Mitigate Risk" for their organizations. Getting everyone in the company to understand these concepts is critical. When all employees fully grasp them, the decisions you make will probably make more sense to them. I always tell my organizations, "You may not like the decision I am making, but I want you to understand the '*why*' behind it."

"Make the Company Money" Case Study

This is a story that I have used throughout my career in leadership development. It's simple, but effective.

My dad was self-employed during most of my childhood, working long hours and often seven days a week. When I was 16 years old, he took a sabbatical from the business world and we moved to our summer cabin that my grandparents had built. During this time, Dad was home every night for dinner, and it was at the dinner table that he taught me about the first part of Tool #1 - "Make the Company Money." That conversation would help me affect the sales revenue of a 30-year-old company.

I had recently started working in a bakery, located in a small California coastal town about 30 minutes north of where I went to high school. This 30-year-old bakery made such wonderful Italian baked goods and specialty breads that customers would travel three hours one way, just to purchase their focaccia and other goodies.

Dad looked across the dinner table at me and asked, "Vicki, what do you want to accomplish with your new job at the bakery?"

"Be the best worker there," I replied. Dad had always taught us that if we were going to do anything, we needed to do our best.

"How do you do that?" he asked.

"By working really hard."

Dad's eyes twinkled as he continued, "Why does Alan own the bakery?"

"Because he likes to bake," I replied.

Dad smiled and asked the question again, "*Why* does he own the bakery?"

This time I replied, "Because he wants to own his own business."

"And why does Alan come to work every day?"

"Because he has to."

By the look on my Dad's face, I knew I wasn't giving him the answer he was looking for. He was patient with me though. He smiled and asked again, "*Why* does Alan have to work?"

I thought about my response this time and said, "So he can make money."

Dad beamed, letting me know that I was on the right track. He continued, "I know you're gonna get this, honey. So, if Alan *has to* make money and you want to be the very best worker for Alan, what do you need to help him with?"

This time the puzzled look on my face was gone. I replied with confidence, "I need to help him make money."

"Now," Dad replied, "we're getting somewhere. *How* can you help Alan make more money?"

"By selling more bread."

"What else?" Dad nudged me forward.

"I can help get people to buy more cookies, donuts, breadcrumbs, and maybe a coffee cake for breakfast the next morning."

"Bingo," said Dad. "You got it! So now the question is, *how* can you get them to buy more baked goods and bread, so Alan can make more money?"

Over the next couple of weeks, Dad taught me some simple "up-selling" techniques. At the bakery, I made notes on the types of bread and other items that ran out early in the day. I would then share the information with Alan and the other bakers, so they could adjust how much of each product they were baking. Over dinner each night, Dad and I went over my notes and brainstormed.

Within a few short months, sales were up at the bakery. Alan rewarded me with a raise, and I couldn't wait to get to work each day. My dad had given me my first understanding of *why* a business is in business. He also taught me how I could be indispensable to my boss. With that knowledge, I have successfully increased revenue for every organization I have ever led in my career. I didn't know it then, but my dad gave me a great gift at a very early age.

"Save the Company Money" Case Study

In most organizations, saving money is critical. This savings can go directly to the bottom line or it can help distribute funds to other initiatives the company is driving. As leaders, we need to help our employees understand that saving the company money is just as important as making the company money.

The president of one of the largest franchises in a global staffing corporation offered me a position to help him increase his revenue. The first office I managed was the largest one in the organization but was barely making enough sales revenue to cover the overhead. I believed that we needed to drive labor and other office costs down while increasing revenue and team productivity. I talked with the team during the weekly staff meeting and explained that we needed to get creative about accomplishing these goals. I knew that performance reviews and compensation raises were scheduled the following month, so I gave them a choice. I could lay off some people to cut payroll costs immediately, or I could keep everyone and freeze their current compensation while we were trying to increase revenue. I explained that when we increased revenue and cut expenses, I would make sure they got their increase in compensation, and also take them to the most expensive restaurant in the city for a celebration lunch. Whatever they decided, I would respect their decision. I gave the team the rest of that day and the weekend to think about it.

When I walked into the meeting room on Monday morning, everyone was there. They all agreed to take the pay freeze and accept my challenge. "Great!" I responded. "That's what I hoped you'd say. Now let's get to work."

At the time, the office was processing six to eight applicants a day through their intake process. I explained to the team that I wanted to process 100 applicants through our system in four hours – without adding additional recruiters or office staff. I explained that we would be able to fill our job orders more quickly and get a jump on our competitors by having a larger number of qualified people in our database who were ready to work. Accomplishing this goal would increase our revenue, increase our market share, and cut down on expenses. I reiterated that, to save money, we had to increase our productivity without hiring additional office employees to help us with this new strategy.

You would have thought that I had told them that I was going to pull their fingernails out. They gasped and emphatically insisted that this was an impossible feat. The office manager asked me how I came up with a goal of 100 applicants. I responded that it just sounded like a big number to shoot for, then turned quickly around to write on the white board so I wouldn't see them rolling their eyes at me. Based on my past experiences, I knew that my passion for the plan and belief in their ability to hit the goal were essential to our success. I could not waiver in that belief. We brainstormed together on how to drive more applicants into our office and how to process them more efficiently. I asked the receptionist to order 30 more chairs for the meeting room since we would have people "pouring into our office doors to apply for jobs the following Monday."

Monday morning arrived, and the meeting room was packed with applicants. Our office lobby was also overflowing with people. I looked out the window and saw people lined up outside the front door of the office building, which presented a different kind of problem. We had planned for 50 applicants, at the most, to filter through the office during the day, but more than 100 people had arrived by 8am.

I walked into the lobby of our office suite and asked the applicants to go outside and wait in the parking lot. I stood on the stairs outside the building and proceeded with my presentation. Even with all the commotion of not being ready for this large group of people, I could feel the excitement and energy within the group that had gathered. After my quick presentation, we asked people to complete an application and come into our office suite for processing. As the applicants walked into our lobby with their completed applications, we realized very quickly that we were not going to be able to process them all with our normal procedures. We modified our plan multiple times during the day, but still could not get people processed quickly enough. My recruiters were literally bumping into each other as they rushed around the office. Eight hours later, the final applicant left the office and I yelled, "Lock the door!"

We stared at one another, looking disheveled and exhausted from the day. We all knew the current process had failed. We didn't process the 100+ applicants who had come in that morning. We couldn't even complete half of them. Some of the applicants left disgusted and I couldn't blame them.

I took the team into the meeting room for debriefing and asked one of them to jump up on the whiteboard to take notes. One by one, we identified the gaps from the day and discussed each of them thoroughly. "The good news is that we now know that we can get 100 people or more here on a Monday morning to apply for our open jobs," I explained. "The bad news is that we don't have an efficient process once they get here." I emphasized my belief in them again and assured them that we would figure out a better process.

The following Monday, we had almost a hundred people show up again. After eight hours, we still were not able to process all of the applicants. By the time we locked the office door at 5pm, a few of my team members were shaking. One of my employees slumped to the floor and cried out, "We'll never be able to do this!"

"Nonsense," I responded. "This was much better. Now, let's debrief and come up with Plan C."

We all walked into the meeting room, just as we had done the week before, and someone started writing the gaps in our process on the whiteboard. We strategized again and left the room with a new draft of our process.

When we locked the door at 5pm on the next Monday, we had processed almost 100 applicants through our office in eight hours. Everyone was energized as they filed into the meeting room for debriefing. Just the fact that we had processed nearly 100 people in eight hours, without panicking or bumping into each other, generated enough excitement to get everyone believing that they could accomplish the overall goal.

Over the next two Mondays, we continuously improved our plan and increased the number of applicants we could move through the process. With each passing week, our job intake process became more efficient. With the business flow improving, you could feel their enthusiasm. Each Monday, someone would yell, "To the meeting room to debrief!" I was no longer in the front of the room leading the discussion. Instead, I sat in the back. I had to smile, as I watched their skill set and confidence grow. The once unattainable goal was now entirely reachable. Based on the number of job orders we filled, the cost per applicant was going down. Revenue was increasing due to more job orders from our clients, which resulted from our ability to fill them more quickly, without bringing additional employees into the office.

On our sixth Monday, armed with our newest process, we opened the doors of our office suite at 8am and by noon we had moved 92 applicants through our process. My team had huge grins on their faces. When the last applicant left about noon and the front door of our office suite was closed, there were screams of excitement. They looked at me in anticipation of my response. I laughed and declared, "Ninety-two is good enough!" Everyone cheered.

In less than six months, sales revenue had doubled, without adding new team members or more labor hours to our budget. We even found a creative way to decrease the budget for our office supplies, when one of my employees jokingly suggested working by candlelight to save on electricity costs! The team's confidence and their leadership skillset increased. In fact, they told me they felt they could accomplish anything. When I announced that performance and compensation discussions were going to be scheduled, they were ecstatic. They each received a bigger increase in their compensation than was initially promised. Their increases also came sooner than expected, because they reached their goal in just under five months.

I asked for their thoughts about the last five months. Responses varied from, "This has changed my career!" to "It feels great to know we can do anything!" Whatever they said, they knew that we had accomplished something great and it was a stepping stone for continued revenue growth toward the president's goals.

I took my team to the most expensive restaurant in the city for lunch and told them they could order anything they wanted. The restaurant rolled out the red carpet for us. For some of my team members, it was their first time dining in that caliber of restaurant and it made a lasting impression on them. One of them asked the server for a copy of the menu, which they proudly displayed on one of the walls in the recruiting bull pen.

Whenever I tell this story, people always ask why I gave the employees the choice of freezing their compensations or layoffs within the organization. By giving the employees a choice, I could explain from a business perspective how I was thinking as a leader. Through the years, I have found that when you are direct with employees, explaining business challenges and options, they will understand what needs to be done. I am not saying they will *like* the decision, but they will *understand why* the decision was made. When that happens, it's easier for people to jump on board with change.

"Mitigate Risk"
Case Study

The third part of Tool #1 is to "Mitigate Risk." Putting your company in jeopardy can negate any gains you make with making money and saving money. In a world of social media, with the ability for information to go viral quickly, mitigating risk is something that all leaders and employees should be acutely aware of. If it isn't adequately evaluated and minimized, companies and their brands can be severely impacted legally and financially.

Just forty-five minutes into my new job at a staffing company, the phone rang. It was one of our largest clients, a Fortune 500 manufacturing company and one of the largest employers in our city. They called and asked to talk with the person in charge. Lilly, the office manager, came in to get me and told me what they were requesting. You don't have to be a genius to know that when a client requests the person in charge, it's probably not good news.

Before taking the call, I asked Lilly how far the client was located from our office. When she responded 20 minutes, I asked her to tell the client that I would personally talk with them in 30 minutes. I then instructed her to grab month over month reporting for the account and meet me in my car. "What do you plan to do?" she asked. I told her I wasn't sure what I was going to say yet, but we were going to go out to the client site and talk with the Vice President of Human Resources, who was the buying influence. She just stared at me and said, "They won't let you in." I smiled, repeated my instructions, and went to my car to wait for her.

Within a few minutes, we were on our way to the client site. Lilly was bringing me up to speed about the client's business and our performance under the contract. She informed me that we had been unable to fill all their job orders on time and with the right candidates. She also reported that we were failing to follow some of our contractual obligations. This put our client's business at risk, which also put our company at risk. I knew losing this top client would be a disaster from a revenue perspective. However, if it leaked that we were putting our client at risk by not following the contract, it would have a more lasting impact, since our franchise company was part of a global company and highly regarded within the city.

We arrived at the client's manufacturing plant and got out of the car. Since I had only been employed at this company for about an hour, I didn't have the right identification badge to get through the client's security. We rehearsed what Lilly would say as we approached the security desk and how we would handle the situation. Armed guards and metal detectors were right in front of me. It was obvious Lilly had built a great relationship with this client because she quickly engaged them in a conversation as we gave them the coffee we had picked up on the way. She did an excellent job on our agreed upon plan and we got through security without any problems.

Once through security, Lilly informed me that the Vice President of Human Resources was located upstairs and that we weren't allowed to go up to that floor. I don't think she was particularly shocked when I said I was taking the elevator upstairs. I told her that she could wait downstairs if she wanted. She responded, "I wouldn't miss this for anything," and quickly followed me into the elevator. We found the office of the Vice President of Human Resources. When we entered the office and introduced ourselves, he immediately began yelling at the top of his voice and his face turned red. I could literally see his jugular vein stick out of the side of his neck. I was afraid he might have a heart attack.

Once he finally finished his rampage, he asked what I wanted. I asked him for another chance and told him we would fix the problem of not getting his job orders filled right away. I also told him that we would ensure all contract requirements were taken care of for each person placed at his plant. He looked at me and said, "You've got to be kidding. I hate your company."

I continued by walking him through my proposed game plan. I looked at him straight in the eye and assured him that I would stake my reputation and my integrity on the fact that we would follow the contract guidelines and get his job orders filled on time, *and* with great candidates. I even told him that if no one was available in our database to show up for work at his manufacturing plant, the people in my office, including myself, would come and work if needed. I ended with the statement, "We won't let you down, I promise."

He reluctantly gave us another chance, and I went back to our office to explain the situation to the team. Someone quickly jumped out of their chair and went to the whiteboard so we could brainstorm. We came up with a quality control plan that encompassed each part of the intake process, thereby mitigating risk.

We promoted a very competent young woman named Eliza to full-time account manager on the account. She was perfect for the position. She was friendly, positive, and had a can-do attitude. Since we were not the exclusive staffing provider for this client, quickly filling the job orders with the right candidates and guaranteeing that we were contractually in alignment was instrumental in getting ahead of our competitors – who were also racing to fill the job orders. We had an opportunity to grow our revenue and repair our reputation with our client at the same time.

While we were working to perfect our intake process, there were a few close calls. At various times, each of the recruiters, account managers, and office team members had to show up and work on the manufacturing line. One day, we received a phone call from the client asking if we could send more people out to the manufacturing plant in short order. Our competitors couldn't assist them, and my team had exhausted all the candidates in our database. They were short one person, and Eliza told me that she needed me to go out there and work. So out to the manufacturing plant I went.

That afternoon, wearing work clothes and a hair net, I stood at one of the food production lines inside the manufacturing plant. As luck would have it, the Vice President of Human Resources was giving some executives a tour and he passed the production line where I was working. He stopped and said, "Vicki, is that you?" I said quickly, "I can't stop and talk, or I will get out of my rhythm here on the line. I promised you I would keep my word and I have."

."You certainly have!" he declared. "Thank you!"

Less than a year later, we had mitigated the company's risk and filled our orders so quickly that they granted us an exclusive contract. The client's human resource department had connected so well with our account manager, Eliza, that we received additional staffing orders for other departments within the company, which further increased our revenue. Streamlining our process to mitigate the risk for our client not only paid off for the client and our company, but also for the hundreds of people we placed in jobs at that manufacturing facility.

Conclusion

"Make Money, Save Money, and Mitigate Risk" are concepts that teach your employees, no matter their experience level, how to bring you better ideas and make better business decisions. This first tool in *The Leadership Toolbox* will also help your employees understand why you make the leadership decisions you make. You will see your team grow in their professional maturity as they develop a leadership mindset. Your employees will reinforce this tool when talking with their peers, which will spread their use throughout your organization. This creates new mindsets that can cultivate better business strategies and help you, as a leader, reach your goals.

Sell the Big Picture
Motivate Employees to Buy into Your Goals

I was 22 years old and working for Leon, a self-made millionaire who made his first million dollars by the time he was 26 years old. He opened his own direct-to-consumer sales company, which financed his favorite habit – buying more real estate. Leon had a flamboyant personality and a commanding presence. People were drawn to him when he walked into the room. Watching people watch him, I realized that his ability to captivate, along with his confidence and motivational style, also gave him the ability to influence.

Leon recruited me to sell in his direct sales company. I started part-time and broke the record for new hire first weekend sales. A few months later, he asked me to lead the new employee sales classes. I agreed and helped increase weekend sales for new hires. As sales revenue continued to grow, Leon decided to scale his business and asked me to help him. It was a fantastic opportunity and I jumped at the chance. Leon increased my salary, gave me a percentage of sales for the entire company, and offered to keep me on a commission scale for new sales people who sold products over their first weekend. My skill set continued to increase, and the company consistently gained momentum, as sales revenue increased rapidly. To this day, I feel fortunate that Leon spent so much time personally mentoring me. He not only helped me increase my leadership mindset and skill set, but he also helped me learn how to run a large sales organization.

Leon explained that leadership was about understanding human behavior. As we worked together each day, he shared his insights on understanding people's feelings and anticipating their reactions to certain business situations. Leon explained that most people yearn to feel good about what they do. I learned that how we lead people can help us quiet their fears and insecurities, increase their excitement, and build their skill sets – all while moving the sales organization forward.

Leon taught me specific strategies for growing a company. I was like a sponge, watching him talk with people and observing how they reacted. His words flowed almost effortlessly, captivating his audience. Leon inspired and motivated people, but most of all, he got them to believe in him and his vision. He convinced them that the team could collectively build a special kind of company that they could play an integral role in. Leon summed it all up one day in the office when he said that people look for a reason to follow a leader and, as leaders, we need to give them a reason to follow us. He said, with a collective belief in the company's vision, we could do great things together.

It was during a discussion one morning that Leon gave me one of the most important tools in *The Leadership Toolbox*. It's the easiest tool to learn, but one with great impact. If you use the tool right, other people in the organization will start using and duplicating it, driving faster positive results. You don't have to instruct people in your organization on how to use the tool. In fact, they won't even know you are using it. They will get excited, buy into what you are driving, and start duplicating your efforts. It's a tool that always works, with huge results.

Leon shared his secret with me. "The secret to building a company is this…" He put his two index fingers together and then separated them. He then moved them straight down and connected them again, drawing a box in the air.

I didn't understand what the heck he was doing, and I must have had a bewildered look on my face. He smiled and said, "The big picture – that's the secret to building a successful business." He looked right at me and kept on smiling. He explained that the big picture was the picture of what the organization was going to look like down the road. It wasn't a mission statement. It wasn't complicated. It was raw and basic. This wasn't just a vision. It was a continuous flow towards that future picture, and it became the second tool in *The Leadership Toolbox*.

Leon explained that you must keep "The Big Picture" in front of people all the time. Not just every month, every week, or every day. Not with signs in the lobby or in everyone's office. You utilize "The Big Picture" with each conversation. I didn't want to argue with him, but that sounded a little over the top to me. Wouldn't people in the organization get sick of hearing the same thing over and over? After the fifth or sixth time of hearing it, wouldn't they start rolling their eyes each time "The Big Picture" was brought up?

Leon must have been inside my head because he said, "It's not about them remembering what you say – it's about them *believing* it. He went on to explain that the confidence in what the organization's success would look like and their place within that organization must become part of the employee's belief system. If it became part of their belief system, then everything they did at work would help drive them toward that goal. If everyone believed and everyone was working toward "The Big Picture," the company would reach its goals faster.

Still, it sounded too simple and it was unrealistic to believe something so simple would work. I started watching Leon recruit and train our sales organization. He talked about "The Big Picture" over and over in group settings, as well as when he talked to individuals. On every phone call, he not only talked about "The Big Picture," he ended every conversation with it. I was shocked and wondered why I hadn't noticed it before. It wasn't like he just started talking about "The Big Picture." He had been talking about it the entire time I worked for him. It was his belief system and I realized that it was already mine, even without knowing that he was deliberately utilizing this tool. "The Big Picture" was now part of the company's belief system as a whole. He told me that people want to believe in something bigger than themselves, and "The Big Picture" helped them realize that desire.

"We are going to be the largest company in the industry."

"We are the fastest growing company in the country."

"We are going to break the national sales record in the industry."

As I watched him recruit and train, I kept track of how many times in a day he would say phrases illustrating "The Big Picture." Some days my tick marks filled up both sides of an 8-1/2 x 11-inch piece of paper. Leon taught me exactly what to say and how to illustrate "The Big Picture." I admit that it felt uncomfortable and forced at the beginning. I was expecting people to roll their eyes, but that never happened. The more I talked about "The Big Picture," the easier it was to talk about it. Soon, it felt completely natural for me and the phrases just rolled off my tongue. My own belief in "The Big Picture" helped me talk about it with conviction.

It amazed me to see how every person in every department believed "The Big Picture." Everyone started talking about it. Everywhere you turned, people were speaking about being the fastest growing company in the industry. They consistently talked about us being the top distributors in our industry. In the hall, in the offices, in the meeting room, out in the field – everyone spoke about how we had the best people and how we were going to the top. We repeatedly broke weekly and monthly sales records, as the company's revenue grew. "The Big Picture" feeling was contagious and there seemed to be no limits to what we could do.

In less than 18 months, we expanded to five offices, built a recruiting and training machine, and developed a way to train new salespeople in the field. We became the largest specialty company of its kind in the country and the fastest growing company in the industry. "The Big Picture" happened, just as Leon said it would. He would sometimes look across the room at me and illustrate "The Big Picture" in the air with his index fingers before smiling and leaving the room.

How can something so simple be so powerful? It wasn't the words themselves, or even the index fingers making a "The Big Picture" box in the air. It was that the people in the organization believed "The Big Picture." It was contagious. The sales meetings grew larger and larger until we outgrew our corporate office space and had to construct our own building. It was fascinating to watch the organization grow so rapidly. It was like a movement – and I was part of it.

The foundation of my leadership style was built during my work with Leon. I am eternally grateful to him for spending so much time mentoring me. He taught me how to keep the organization's future vision in front of the people at all times, a tool that has become a habit for me. Today, it's a natural part of my leadership style and part of me. My employees consistently utilize "The Big Picture" word choices. It's also impacted my clients, who sometimes even repeat "The Big Picture" to me.

This feeling of being a part of something bigger than yourself is at the core of most start-ups. Employees believe that their creation of the newest widget, social media platform, or retail strategy will change the world. Everyone gets caught up in the momentum, and soon the employees feel unstoppable. Look at Apple, Google, Amazon, and a host of other companies that started small and grew into mega corporations with a major impact on the world. However, you don't have to be LinkedIn or Facebook to have that same type of momentum inside your company.

Case Study

One summer day my phone rang. It was a senior director from a business process outsourcing company (BPO). They had a contract with a Fortune 100 company to answer customer support phone calls for the holiday season and they were in trouble. Their customer service satisfaction scores were far below the required 85% and the client was threatening to cancel their contract.

The story was all too familiar. The Fortune 100 company had given the BPO an ultimatum and suggested they contact me for help, since I had assisted another one of their vendors the previous year. The BPO had already lost millions of dollars in less than six months and without this contract, they had no chance of recouping that loss. Turning the situation around would mean renewed confidence from the client and the potential for millions of dollars in new business.

Less than an hour into our conversation, the BPO offered me the job. While I appreciate being "so wanted," I knew from experience that when a business is in trouble, senior-level leadership seldom knows the full extent of the challenges. Further complicating matters, this BPO had absolutely no experience in the 100% virtual/work at home environment, which is managed entirely different than traditional brick and mortar contact centers.

The following week, I flew to their international headquarters and talked with the Senior Vice President, Senior Director, and department heads. After a few hours of asking questions, it was obvious to me that this problem could not be solved by tweaking a few operational procedures. To be successful, we literally needed to turn around and rebuild the organization. With millions of dollars already lost and millions of dollars on the line, this BPO needed to move fast if it was to stay in business and keep hundreds of employees working. It would be like rebuilding a fast-moving train – while it was moving and with a team that didn't know how to properly operate it. The revenue for the entire division of this global company rested with the revenue of this one client.

The SVP wanted me to move them into the range of average customer service satisfaction scores so they could keep the account, but I don't believe in being average and I wasn't interested in that approach. I told him that I would only take the job if moving the organization to number one out of 22 international vendors was the goal. It was all or nothing for me. If they couldn't get on board, I couldn't be their new leader. The executives ultimately agreed, and I got to work turning this BPO around.

I wasn't surprised to find a lack of honest communication between the business units and the executive team. After all, if the business units knew what to do, they would do it. Instead, executives sometimes stick their heads in the sand and hope things will take care of themselves, or they expect that the management teams will miraculously gain new skills and get better results. After digging through reports, I discovered employee attrition was over 400% annualized, customer satisfaction scores were at 59%, and employee absenteeism was 25% per day.

I grabbed *The Leadership Toolbox* and immediately put "The Big Picture" tool to work. For me, "The Big Picture" was about two goals: achieving the number one placeholder in customer service satisfaction scores among 22 other vendors and beating the client's own internal customer support teams. I was fanatical about using "The Big Picture" tool, starting and ending every conversation with phrases like "We're going to the TOP" and "We're going to be number one." Every one of my emails started and ended with "The Big Picture."

To further communicate "The Big Picture," I produced three to five videos per week for the operations teams across the country. I talked about "The Big Picture" multiple times in every video and ended each one with "See you at the TOP!" My videos were forwarded to other divisions within the company, sparking an international corporate rally behind the team and me.

Driving the strategic plan, we saw great improvement in customer service satisfaction scores within a couple of months, but nowhere near our goal of number one in customer service satisfaction scores (CSATs). However, the Fortune 100 client was encouraged by our improvement and the contract was saved. The executive team breathed a huge sigh of relief. Financially, we were still in the red.

Even with this success, I kept driving "The Big Picture." By now, all levels of leadership and front-line agents saw the upward momentum and started to believe. We put in new processes and new coaching plans. I built a hybrid version of self-directed teams inside the organization. By now, we had grown to over 500 agents and slowly climbed to the number one spot internationally. Customer support agents had "See you at the TOP" in their email signature lines. "We're going to be number one" was a common "The Big Picture" phrase heard over and over by the hundreds of front-line customer support agents during team meetings. I did virtual town halls with every group of new agents before they took customer calls. I gave a short 20-minute presentation that was chock-full of "The Big Picture" statements. I would then open the virtual floor up to questions and comments. I routinely heard new agents declare how excited they were to be with an organization that was going to the top. The client's vendor manager started telling me that he believed we would be number one, and even our company SVP called me one morning to say that we were "going to the top!"

Five months from the day I walked through the door, this virtual/work at home national contact center hit number one in customer service satisfaction scores, during the busiest week of call volume for the year – between Christmas and New Year's Day. You could feel the energy from the excitement of the agents and leadership, even in a virtual/work at home environment! People told me that they could feel the excitement in the chat rooms. The entire organization buzzed. I was at the Fortune 100 client site in California when I heard the news. When I walked into the meeting room, their managers gave me a standing ovation. Even they were amazed at what we had accomplished.

Once we hit the number one spot in CSATs, my agents and leadership teams believed we could do anything. We were consistently one of the top-performing vendors for our Fortune 100 client. One year, we recruited and trained 1,400 additional advisors in just 90 days and had great key performance indicators. We also built a new flex virtual site with 300 brand new agents in less than six weeks, utilizing one operations manager and seven top front-line advisors who were leadership development candidates. The site did so well that the client asked us to keep it open for five months.

The first two months we had average key performance indicators – even while operating with *only new advisors*. In the third, fourth, and fifth months, this 300-seat virtual/work at home flex site with brand new advisors and only one formal leader was receiving performance bonuses, outperforming other vendors' internal team and veteran contact center sites.

To draw a quick comparison, the Fortune 100 client's internal contact center teams had outstanding health insurance, stock options, and other corporate benefits. Their front-line technology advisors made 40% more compensation than my front-line employees did. Conversely, my employees were temporary employees, with no health benefits, no 401K, and no stock options. The client started asking questions about what we were doing to drive improvements and requested I talk with various leaders within their organization.

I developed an "on-the-ground" leadership development program and new mentoring initiatives based on *The Leadership Toolbox*. All programs cultivated new leadership, so we were ready for growth. It seemed like everything the organization tackled, we excelled at doing. It built momentum. We were doing it new and different. The results were there, and everyone was excited.

In less than 18 months from when I walked in the door, the organization earned back the millions of dollars it had lost, and we posted a profit to the bottom line. The executive team was ecstatic. They confided in me that they never believed moving to top status within the client's international vendor organization was even possible. I stayed a couple of more years and we built the organization to over 2,000 people. We received performance bonuses on multiple key performance indicators month after month after month. The client repeatedly told me that they couldn't believe we accomplished so much while still growing at a rapid pace.

People ask me if "The Big Picture" was the real reason we went to the top. I tell them it's one of the tools that helped us get there. It's the most important in my opinion and it amazes me to watch front-line employees embrace "The Big Picture" for their organization. They get excited about coming to work, so employee absenteeism and attrition decrease. When employees are excited, they talk faster, so productivity increases. They do a better job, so the customers are happy. For this BPO, reducing employee absenteeism, reducing employee attrition, and increasing customer service satisfaction scores increased their revenue and bottom line contribution.

Tips for Gaining Traction and Achieving Results While Using "The Big Picture"

- Start every discussion with "The Big Picture." Then, mention it again during the discussion and at the end. For coaching sessions or longer discussions, make sure you interject it three or four times.

- "The Big Picture" tool should be emphasized thousands of times by many different people. By duplicating your efforts, the goal will gain traction quickly.

The momentum starts with you as the leader. You don't have to instruct others to use this second tool in *The Leadership Toolbox*. As a leader, if you use "The Big Picture" tool over and over, others will start using it and your effort will be multiplied. You simply do your part as a leader, and you can gain momentum.

"The Big Picture" Conversation Examples

Ralph: "Hey Bob, how's it going?"

Bob: "Going great, Ralph. How are things with you?"

Ralph: "Good on my end, too. Hey, I wanted to ask you a quick question about the phone system. We were talking about some issues in my staff meeting today. If we're going to be number one, my team is a little concerned about some of the gaps we are seeing on continuity."

Bob: "Yeah, that could be a real issue. Why don't we get a quick 15-minute teleconference together and walk through things? We don't want that causing an issue. As we go to the top, those gaps could dilute our success and cause us to miss the goal."

Ralph: "Why don't you send me some times that you and your team are available next week, and I'll send out the invite."

Bob: "Will do. We'll get to the top! Thanks, Ralph. Talk with you soon."

"The Big Picture" Email Example

Hi Sue,

Hope your day is going well. As we are *driving towards the number one spot*, I'm concerned about the rumors that our health insurance premiums are going to go up next year. This is a real sensitive subject for the employees.

I was wondering if we could schedule some time to have a discussion next week. I'm available Monday afternoon, early Wednesday morning, and Thursday in the afternoon from 2:30pm to 4pm MST. Any of those times work for you?

We need to come up with an approach, both strategically and tactically, to address the employees' concerns. We don't want them to be distracted about this issue, get afraid and have them take their eye off *the goal of being number one*.

Thanks for your help.

Vicki

"The Big Picture" can be used at all levels in the organization – from CEO to the front-line employees. Utilizing "The Big Picture" in these types of conversations, emails and meetings, and teleconferences will multiply your effort and can help you gain momentum moving forward.

Leadership Development – Other Ways to Utilize "The Big Picture"

In one of my organizations, I asked my direct reports to count how many times I utilized "The Big Picture" in my videos, emails, texts, and phone calls. When I asked them what they had observed in my communication, they all said they were amazed to see how much I talked about "The Big Picture." Awareness within all levels of your leadership team will help multiply your efforts even faster. Newsletters, videos, emails, sales contests, employee surveys, team meetings, and banners on your intranet are all places that "The Big Picture" can be used. Don't forget other departments, such as: Human Resources, Quality Control, Compliance, Recruiting, Training, Warehouse, Shipping and Receiving, Marketing, Procurement, Legal, Finance, and yes, the IT department. Remember, everyone is a human being, and everyone wants to be a part of something bigger than themselves.

In one of my organizations, I offered points every time a first or second-level leader mentioned "The Big Picture" in a meeting. For every point, they got one entry into a drawing for a gift card or some other small prize. Be creative and make it fun for the greatest impact.

In another company, one of my directors wanted his first, second and third-level leaders to role-play utilizing "The Big Picture." In my opinion, one of the biggest travesties with corporate training is that it is mostly theory. Very little time is spent role-playing or repeatedly practicing a technique. I had never done this before, so I was anxious to see everyone's reaction. It was a success. These leaders loved doing it, and as my mom always said, "Practice makes perfect."

Driving Change with "The Big Picture" – Not Tug of War!

People say they like change. However, when it's time to make necessary changes, they feel uncomfortable and suddenly find numerous reasons why the new way won't work. "The Big Picture" tool minimizes, and even eliminates, the tug of war that comes along with trying to get employees to change. When a leader can truly implement "The Big Picture" belief system, employees drive themselves toward the goal. Why have one leader struggling to pull people forward, when you can have hundreds or thousands of people wanting to move forward on their own?

Key Performance Indicators and "The Big Picture"

I have used "The Big Picture" for 20 years in every organization I have consulted with or led with phenomenal results. Examples include:

- Sales revenue, sales conversion, and customer service satisfaction scores were increased, along with a long list of key performance indicators that affect the bottom line of the company every single time.

- Within 90 days, almost effortlessly changed the culture of an organization from customer service environment to a consultative sales environment where the employees insisted they were not sales people and could not sell anything.

- Employees reduced expenses without complaining, because they felt part of the solution to drive the organization towards "The Big Picture."

- Front-line employees were more willing to change their schedules because of their belief in "The Big Picture."

- Employees were energized at work and they showed up, so absenteeism was slashed.

- Employee attrition was cut in half or more, saving thousands or millions of dollars.

- Companies doubled and tripled in size, when the people truly wanted to achieve "The Big Picture."

Belief in "The Big Picture" is the foundation of moving any organization forward. If we believe something, then our actions reflect that belief and performance improves.

Everyone Has a Sign on Their Head That Says, 'Make Me Feel Important'
Engage Employees Through Honest Dialogue

Terri had built a very successful direct sales organization for Mary Kay Cosmetics and had recently moved from Texas to Missouri. When she applied for a management position in our direct to consumer sales organization, Leon and I thought she would be a great addition to the team. With her mountains of energy and straight to the point approach, people just gravitated to her.

During one Monday morning sales meeting, Leon asked Terri to provide the group with some tips for increasing their personal sales. Her philosophy was that before you can sell anything to a prospective customer, you must help them get to a place where they are willing to receive that information. This, Terry went on to explain, isn't just about building rapport. It is also about acknowledging something positive about the person, even before starting the rapport-building process. She said that helping make someone feel important opens them up to receive the information you want to convey, but she also offered a warning. To make a person truly feel important, they must feel your sincerity. If people think you are not being sincere, they will not hear anything you say and will not trust your information. They won't purchase your product if they don't trust you.

As I watched Terri communicate with others, I observed how she always had a positive word for each person. I watched each person's reaction when she spoke to them. There were smiles. Some would even stand a little taller or sit up in their chair as she talked with them. Her approach seemed effortless. Terri had taken this concept and created a life-long habit that was a key component to her own personal style and, ultimately, her professional success.

Later that afternoon, I was sitting at my desk staring out the window while mulling over Terri's concept and trying to come up with a visual based on her technique. I came up with a concept where there was an imaginary cloud between myself and each person I met. By using Terri's strategy of saying something to help make the person feel important, I could remove the gray cloud and have a meaningful conversation. I knew this wasn't just about saying thank you to a person. It was about acknowledging something positive about them as a human being. How would my organization feel and perform if each person felt validated? Would they show up to work and feel more engaged to serve each other and their customers? Would they feel more comfortable to come up with cost saving measures for the company? Would they be more apt to come up with new services that could serve customers or clients and increase sales revenue?

I realized that if my entire organization could feel validated, they would feel empowered to contribute in some way to the company's success. Through the years, I have realized that the fastest way to achieve change within an organization starts with people feeling good about themselves. This is an extremely important realization, especially if your company is going through significant changes.

Today, I use this tool in almost all of my conversations. It has become a life-long habit and an effective tool for opening the door, so that honest dialogue can happen, and people can be more receptive to what I am saying. Through the years, I have shared this tool with many people. Several have commented that individuals might grow tired of hearing something positive about themselves every time you talk with them. That hasn't been my experience though. People never grow tired of hearing positive words about themselves. They actually crave them.

Let's do a little math and see how utilization of this tool can quickly impact your team's performance and cause a chain reaction of success in the organization. As a leader, if you talk to 10 people a day and utilize this tool, and each of those people meet five people and utilize this tool, you will have influenced 60 people in your organization. If just five of those 60 people each use this tool with five other employees, you now have had an impact on 85 people across the enterprise. If we duplicate those efforts over and over by making people feel validated, how will they perform at work? Try this for one day with everyone you come in contact with – in person, in chat, in text, and on the phone. Notice how people react. Then, take it a step further. Make a further commitment and utilize this tool for one week. You will actually feel the energy and see attitudes in your departments, teams, and company change. Over time, your employees will utilize the "Everyone Has a Sign on Their Head That Says, 'Make Me Feel Important'" tool when they interact with others, creating an even larger impact.

Case Study

I was hired by the president of a contact center company to launch a new service offering. He was convinced that this offering, a new lead generation program, would bring huge amounts of revenue into the company. He felt that this service would be a great way to introduce clients to our company and help move them to the next level with their sales and revenue goals. It was his belief that once the clients saw our significant results, they would increase the number of services purchased from our company.

The IT department had developed the software for this program before I was hired. Since our service offering was something new in the industry, they had developed what they thought would be needed. However, the software wasn't customizable for each client, which proved frustrating for the clients and my teams. Since I am fanatical about the level of service I give my clients, we had to create all types of "work-arounds" in order to accommodate for this static piece of software.

Scott, the Vice President of IT in our company, was a professional, calm-under-pressure, and fair leader. His people liked working in his department, which had very little employee attrition. At this point, I had been with the company about eight months. We had taken on client after client, and our bottom line contribution was increasing month over month. Client satisfaction was almost at 100%. Everything was going well, except for the fact that the developed software still lacked customization, which meant that my team had to spend a lot of extra time on workarounds each day.

My contact center agents were resourceful and started trying to add customization by utilizing an old-fashioned way of keeping track of changes. They used Post-it notes. The team even got "sophisticated" by using different colors and sizes for each client, so that they could quickly access the information. These Post-it notes were all around the outside of their computer monitors. We even had clipboards to tally ad hoc results for clients. Our clients understood our limitations and that our IT department was working diligently on the issue to try to make the software application customizable. They were appreciative of our archaic processes, even though there was human error in the provided information.

I had daily discussions about our software with Scott, and our discussions became quite passionate. There was mutual respect; however, I was pushing him to work faster, so that we could help our clients and their customers. It seemed like a constant tug of war every day. Neither one of us budged. I was pushing hard and he was pushing back, saying he was moving as fast as he could. I knew that he and his team were working hard, but I was looking for the magic wand to take away all the problems and help me service my clients, while he was being logical and didn't believe in magic wands. With each conversation, I opened *The Leadership Toolbox*. The first tool I utilized with him was always "Everyone Has a Sign on Their Head That Says, 'Make Me Feel Important.'" This wasn't hard to do because he had a lot of great qualities and his department was instrumental in driving the company's success.

Late one afternoon, one of my clients requested that we inform each caller about an open house scheduled for the following month. He was looking for feedback and reaction from his potential customer about the open house announcement. I told him, "Of course." My organization took to the Post-it note brigade, using the notes as a reminder to tell each customer about the open house. We then used "tick sheets" to tally up the responses and give the client ad hoc reporting on how many respondents planned to attend. This is not the way to run a business. It puts stress on employees, and the reported numbers are never accurate. Even with our software limitations, we had a reputation of making things happen for our clients. The Post-it note stop gap was out of control and we needed the IT department to provide that magic wand.

I thought all night about how I was going to approach Scott in the morning. I knew when he found out about the open house arrangement, he would be upset. It was just one more customizable field on the software application to put on the project management schedule. I needed to think out of the box for this round with him. I decided I would get up at 4am and make a batch of my famous banana nut bread. Right before I left the house, I took the bread out of the oven, wrapped the hot loaf of bread in foil, and surrounded it with a big fluffy bath towel. I also packed freshly whipped butter in a small crystal bowl, a couple of plates, a sterling silver bread knife, and some napkins. I knew this was a little over the top, but I thought it might take the edge off what I perceived would be a really heated discussion between the two of us.

I got to the office at 6am and told the morning team that I was expecting Scott to show up at my office door. I asked the team to let me know when they saw him barreling down the operations floor toward my office. About 45 minutes later, someone stepped into my office and said, "He's on his way. He's mad. His face is red. I can see his jugular vein popping out of his neck."

For months, in every conversation I had utilized "Everyone Has a Sign on Their Head That Says, 'Make Me Feel Important'" from *The Leadership Toolbox*. I always acknowledged him on something, either professionally about him or his department. I meant every word I had said in each interaction. Since our division was growing so rapidly, I knew the stress on every department was extremely high, especially the IT department. In the first place, Scott knew that his team had developed the software code to be static and not customizable before the CEO had hired me. Second, I knew his team was working diligently on changing that but that it was too slow in coming for the speed at which we were growing.

I glanced out my door. We had an open floor plan and I could see him walking extremely fast toward my office. Even from far away, I could see his red face. It was obvious that he was very upset with me. As Scott walked in my office, I stood up and said, "Good morning." He closed my office door and started pacing. Back and forth he paced across my office, back and forth, back and forth. Mad was an understatement and I waited for him to speak first.

He stopped pacing, looked straight at me, and said, "You make me so damn mad. I have tried to hate your guts, but I can't because you are so damn nice." He stood there looking at me.

I was tempted to crack a small joke to lighten up the mood, but quickly ruled out that option and said the next best thing: "I baked some banana nut bread early this morning. It's still warm. Would you like some?"

"That would be nice," he replied. He sat down on the other side of my desk. I sliced him some bread and asked him if he would like some whipped butter on it. He said, "Yes." I put a slice of warm bread on a plate, spread butter on it, and handed him the plate. He just looked at me, trying to calm down. He took a bite of bread and said, "Vicki, I know your heart is in the right place with the clients, and I know we developed the software not to be customized, which was a big mistake. I know we have to fix this, but you are driving me crazy."

I said to him, "We are on the same page. How do you suppose we fix this?" Over a couple of slices of warm banana bread, I opened *The Leadership Toolbox* and picked out multiple tools:

- We were changing the industry with our new service offering. ("The Big Picture")

- Our business development team was bringing in client after client after client. We needed changes quickly to our software. We needed to get creative on moving up our timelines for that to be completed so we could increase our gross revenue even more. ("Make Money")

- We also had risk if the data was not correct on the reporting. ("Mitigate Risk")

- Even though my team was excited about our new business model, the changes were still stressful. My employee attrition was only at three percent annualized, but I was worried I would have turnover, which would cost more recruiting and training dollars. ("Save Money")

- He was the subject matter expert on technology. I wasn't. I was counting on him to figure this out because he was smart and had a great team. ("Everyone Has a Sign on Their Head That Says, 'Make Me Feel Important'")

He looked at me and smiled. "Okay," he said, "we'll get creative. Can we meet later today?"

I smiled, thanked him, and apologized for pushing him so hard. He looked me square in the eye and said, "You're doing what you're supposed to be doing. You are taking care of the clients and helping them grow their businesses. I'm disappointed because we're not moving fast enough for you."

That afternoon, I sat in his office as he laid out a new plan. He had figured out a way to speed up the project. There were other departments with bigger needs all over the company, but I truly believe that all the months of utilizing "Everyone Has a Sign on Their Head That Says, 'Make Me Feel Important'" kept putting deposits into his bank. Every one of those acknowledgements I gave him was sincere. I meant every one of them. We utilized the tool in his department as well. We put up signs in the department saying, "Thank You." We made sure each member received a birthday card. We brought them goodies to munch on and invited them to our potlucks.

The new change in our software application led to more customizable reporting. In fact, we could make immediate changes intra-day and start reporting on them, which gave our clients more opportunities in their businesses to increase revenue. It was a major change that reaped huge rewards for our division and company.

Our division went on to grow and to post record profits, and the new service offering influenced the way the entire industry cultivated their lead flow. We not only took on more clients, but our division became the incubator for business within our company. By understanding our clients' businesses, we could engage them in more services from our company. Everyone won – our company, the client's company, and the customers we talked to on the phone. Our employees were given opportunities for advancement, and the IT team grew as well, moving their top front-line team members into leadership positions. Everybody won.

Practice Creates a Habit That Drives Success

When you make people feel acknowledged and validated, they are more receptive to what you are saying because it removes that gray cloud from between you and the other person. By multiplying this feeling across your company, more people are acknowledged in every conversation, email, chat, and text. A strong habit is created that not only can enhance the culture in your organization but can dramatically turn around performance, revenue, and even line items on your budget. In my companies, whether in brick and mortar facilities or in a virtual/work at home environment, you can actually feel the energy, as well as see the results.

All the tools in *The Leadership Toolbox* are building blocks for each other. By utilizing multiple tools in each interaction, you can multiply the effect. Others will emulate your actions. Use of these tools will have a snowball effect in your organization and you will be able to feel and see the difference in your people and their performance.

Dangle the Carrot
Understand What Motivates Your People and Capitalize on It

Most people believe that compensation is the main driver of low employee attrition rates. However, study after study has demonstrated that this is not the case. In fact, I've done the research, and I could not find a single study to support the claim that compensation is a key indicator of low employee attrition. Consider these statistics:

- A recent Gallup poll stated that 51% of U.S. workers overall were considering looking for a new job.

- A Korn Ferry Survey of executives recently found that 90% of executives reported that keeping new hires was an issue in their organization.

- Keeping employees engaged is one of the top three challenges facing companies, as reported by a recent SHRM survey.

Employee engagement is a hot topic for company executives and leadership. But how do you engage employees so they want to stay and do a great job while helping you reach your goals?

Leon, my mentor early in my career, was a master at understanding people. Under his mentoring, I learned how to engage and motivate people toward success. He understood the inherent need to conquer or accomplish something, and even though I had heard the phrase "Dangle the Carrot" for years, Leon took that concept to a whole new level.

I must admit that the first time I heard Leon say the words "Dangle the Carrot" it sounded almost disrespectful, like it was a game. Sensing my discomfort, he went on to explain that we all chase the "carrots" in our lives. For some people, it's the thought of buying the new house, a fancy car, or a second home. To some, it's about power, prestige, or achieving a social media following. For others, the carrot is to get to the top, run the marathon, or feel good about losing weight. Leon explained that each person is motivated by different "carrots." There are employees that show up and do just enough to keep their jobs and their "carrot" is their paycheck. But how far can an organization advance when filled with those types of workers?

Great leaders understand that employees need a goal or specific achievement to work toward in order to deliver at peak performance. If there is nothing to work for, it is human nature just to show up and move through your tasks. Productivity will eventually decrease for this type of employee. So as a leader, understanding what motivates your employees can be the key to driving phenomenal results. Keeping that motivation in front of them every day will help them on those days when they are frustrated, tired, or when things aren't going well personally or professionally. When employees are engaged and working towards a goal, you can build momentum in your organization. That's when things can really happen to move your company forward.

I noticed that Leon mentioned those "carrots" each time he talked with one of his employees. Just as he had repeated "The Big Picture" over and over, I saw him "Dangle the Carrot" over and over. Again, I thought this was over the top, but as I watched people's body language and facial expressions, I realized that they were buying into their own "carrots." Leon just reminded them of what they were working for. It was the hope of what was to come, when we buckle down and work hard.

I have a friend on Facebook whom I first met in the fifth grade. Every morning she posted a picture of herself walking around the mall. I had no idea why she was posting these pictures every day, and it went on for months, with everyone cheering her on. One day, she posted a picture of herself in a retail store standing in front of a three-part mirror, showing off her thinner body in a pair of jeans. It dawned on me that the "carrot" was fitting into a certain size pair of jeans and her friends on Facebook helped keep that "carrot" out in front of her by cheering her on.

As a leader, I want to help my employees reach their goals. I take a personal stake in their "carrots" when I acknowledge what their goals are in each interaction I have with them, whether it's in person, on the phone, in a chat, on the company social media platform, or in a text. The "Dangle the Carrot" tool in *The Leadership Toolbox* helps keep me focused on what my employees' goals are, so that I can support them by encouraging them, by mentoring or coaching them, and by moving obstacles out of their way so they can achieve what they want.

Case Study

Kevin has worked with me in several different companies and consulting engagements. He is a senior leader and a student of human behavior in business. Today he has mastered the tools in *The Leadership Toolbox*, but he was not always this type of leader. In fact, he was on the verge of being terminated from the first organization I worked with him in.

Kevin was a first-level supervisor when I met him. He was all business, and there was no room in his conversations for even a hint of caring for his employees. He believed that business was business and personal was personal. He barked orders and didn't take time to listen to anyone on his own team or any of the other managers, for that matter. Kevin's employees were constantly hanging over their cubicles in the office talking with other supervisors. This would infuriate Kevin. He would reprimand these employees publicly and demand that they sit down. Some of his employees would even break down and cry right on the operations floor. I also observed these same employees talking with other supervisors in the hall or break room.

On one occasion, I overheard one of Kevin's direct reports sharing one of her ideas with another supervisor. His employees seemed to be upset with him about something and some even asked to change teams. I also noticed that other supervisors didn't want to work with Kevin on projects, and it was hard for him to get group collaboration in the supervisor meetings. Kevin's inability to speak with people respectfully or to build rapport within the organization affected every facet of his job.

Kevin's immediate manager spoke with him and coached him several times, yet each time he was approached with something he needed to change, Kevin blamed someone else. Nothing was ever his fault. There were even several discussions within my management team about terminating Kevin's employment. He didn't match the culture in the organization. We were at our wits end on what to do with him and it was sad to see someone with so much potential on the verge of losing his job.

One day, I was on the contact center floor talking with the agents. Some of Kevin's agents were hanging over the wall, eager to talk with me. One of them was excited to share a new sales concept with me. Kevin marched right up and told this agent to sit down. Everyone looked shocked that Kevin would do this right in front of me. I thanked everyone for their time and continued walking the operations floor.

Because I had firsthand knowledge of Kevin's interaction, I thought I would try a different approach with him. It was actually more like a last-ditch effort to see if I could help him keep his job. I found out what shift Kevin worked the next day and made sure I was near the entrance to the building when he arrived for work. When I saw him, I waved. He waved back and maneuvered his way over to where I was standing. We chitchatted for a few minutes, and then I asked him what he liked best about working in the contact center. He said he liked being a supervisor, but that he really wanted to be promoted to the next level. Once he told me that, I understood that a promotion was his "carrot." I asked Kevin if he would like my assistance on a game plan for getting a promotion. He was all smiles and enthusiastically agreed. I told Kevin I would have time for a mentoring moment later that afternoon, and we set an appointment for him to come to my office.

When I got to my desk, I called his direct manager and told him what had happened. I wanted to make sure that the manager heard it from me and not from Kevin. Even though I placed that call the minute I got to my desk, Kevin was already on the operations floor telling everyone in the organization that he was going to be mentored by me that afternoon. Later that morning, I heard that he threatened one of his employees by telling her that if she didn't take another shift, he was going to mention it to me during our meeting. Poor Kevin…he just didn't get it.

That afternoon Kevin and I sat down to have our discussion. I had decided to use my mentoring moment as a brainstorming meeting. Here's where I decided to utilize the "Dangle the Carrot" tool. I had put the title of our discussion at the top of the whiteboard and underlined it. It said, "Kevin's game plan to get promoted!" He loved it.

I gave Kevin the dry-erase marker and said, "Okay, let's come up with a game plan." Kevin smiled and then started writing down some of the details on my whiteboard:

"Make everyone take overtime to help with call volume."

"Make people change their shifts when we need them to."

"Make people get 100 percent CSATs on returned calls."

"Increase sales conversion on the team by 10 percent."

I stopped him and asked how he was going to hit the goals he had just written. He started to explain to me that he needed to move the current agents off his team and get new agents, so that he could hit his goals. I stopped him dead in his tracks. I had two chairs in front of my desk. I pointed to one of them and said, "Let's talk through this and see what we can come up with." Kevin sat down, and I walked around my desk to sit in the chair next to him.

I opened *The Leadership Toolbox* and started with "The Big Picture" tool. I told him that we were going to be the best site in the entire organization. Next, I pulled out the "Make Money" tool and explained that our sales conversion would make the company a lot of money and help us with expansion. I then pulled out the "Everyone Has a Sign on Their Head That Says, 'Make Me Feel Important'" tool. I told him that I thought his analytical style was an asset to the organization (which was true) and that I admired his dedication (which was also true). Now I had his attention and he was open to what I would say next.

Next, I pulled out the "Dangle the Carrot" tool. I asked him if he would be open to me helping him get better at his job, so that he could gain more visibility and work toward his goal of promotion. Kevin nodded. I was still holding the "Dangle the Carrot" and "The Big Picture" tools in my hand as I went on. I explained that because the company was expanding, we would need more managers and that would mean more opportunity for leaders who had shown they could inspire and lead groups of people to get results. I painted a picture for Kevin on how he could learn new skills that would expand his leadership abilities. I mentioned the committees that would drive new ideas and that some of the new managers, middle managers, and senior managers would be working directly with me on numerous initiatives as we expanded our operation.

I went back to the whiteboard and drew a vertical line on the right side of where Kevin had listed what he had to do to get promoted. I wrote "Action Plan" at the top of the right-hand side column and we started to brainstorm. I spent one hour with Kevin, and I talked to him about all of the issues I had observed. When he started to argue with me, I once again opened *The Leadership Toolbox* and pulled out all the tools I had used previously.

We were working toward being the best site in the organization. ("The Big Picture")

We were going to make more money, expand, and have more opportunities for expansion. ("Make Money" and "The Big Picture")

I mentioned that he was smart and would be able to learn new tools. I also informed him that I had all the confidence in the world in him. ("Everyone Has a Sign on Their Head That Says, 'Make Me Feel Important'")

I told him that, once he developed new skills, he would be able to teach others to take his place as a supervisor, so that he could move up the ladder to the next level of leadership. ("Dangle the Carrot")

I then paused and looked straight into his eyes. I said to him, "Kevin, it's up to you to change your behavior and be the kind of leader that people want to work with." I waited for him to speak. It was a long pause.

He shifted around in his chair and quietly said, "Okay, I will try." I continued to look Kevin straight in the eye. It looked like he wasn't even breathing. I asked him to trust me and assured him that if he tried and mastered these new skills, people would want to be in his organization.

I watched Kevin struggle to change his behavior over the following weeks. It was clear from his body language that the changes did not come easily. He was obviously uncomfortable at times, but I could see him working through the challenges. However, true to human nature and repetition of the tools in *The Leadership Toolbox*, the employees noticed his efforts and eventually began to appreciate his new attitude. The team recognized his new leadership style and he started to win them over! I, along with other managers and my senior managers, watched in amazement as one by one, the employees on his team got behind him. He literally changed before our eyes.

Some months later, as we were expanding, it was obvious to everyone that Kevin was the person to be promoted. He had nailed the tools in *The Leadership Toolbox* and his "carrot" was delivered. When his promotion was announced, his team cheered! People crowded around him to congratulate him and his team was genuinely excited.

The afternoon after Kevin received his promotion, he came into my office, sat down in front of my desk, and cried. He was so grateful. It was also a special moment for me as I teared up. I had watched him struggle. I had watched him fall flat on his face and get up. His managers and I were there with him every step of the way, reinforcing the tools from *The Leadership Toolbox*. He did the work, and it paid off.

Through the years, I have consistently used the "Dangle the Carrot" tool, and I want to stress that it must be an honest "carrot." If, for any reason, people think they are being used or manipulated, they will lose interest and respect for you. If that happens, it's unlikely you will make it across the finish line, since your team will not be anywhere in sight. Honesty must be part of the "carrot." As my mentor Leon put it, you must be sincere, or it won't work.

Utilizing *The Leadership Toolbox* with Front-Line Employees

People have asked me for years, "Why do you spend time with front-line employees? How do you have the time to do that?" I always smile when I get these questions. What do you think the front-line employees and supervisors say when I work with someone on the front lines? Do you think they are silent and don't say anything? The news spreads like wild fire. It makes me look more human. Other people start watching what's going on, and behaviors start to change. I have seen excitement spread throughout the organization in both brick and mortar and virtual/work-at-home environments when I spend time mentoring, talking to, or coaching front-line employees. The information shared during these communications helps the entire organization. Being visible on the front lines has a direct effect on how fast the organization moves forward. I can influence greater numbers of people in the organization and achieve phenomenal results more quickly.

When working in a virtual/work at home environment, coaching, mentoring, and conversations go viral within 15 seconds. When I mention working with a front-line employee on the company social media page or the company intranet, it drives excitement across the entire organization and I get more traction on my rapid turnaround and strategic plan growth. I've been doing this for years, and it works every time.

Case Study
"Dangling the Carrot" for Your Entire Organization

If you are a leader, even one with multiple layers of leaders reporting to you, then you can optimize the "Dangle the Carrot" tool in *The Leadership Toolbox* to benefit your entire organization.

I had an opportunity to lead a turnaround in a virtual / work at home contact center organization. At the time of my arrival at the company, employee attrition was over 300% annualized. The bottom line showed a loss of millions of dollars since launching the business unit earlier that year. This organization answered the phones for a Fortune 500 client and part of their contract with this client was to ramp up the size of their organization during large product launches and seasonal surges in call volume. I systematically worked through a multitude of challenges in this organization when I first arrived. However, we continued to have the challenge of getting enough agents to sign up for additional phone hours after the overtime schedules were posted. Our client kept asking for additional phone hours and I was constantly posting videos, asking my front-line team for assistance by taking more hours on their schedules.

These large product launches and seasonal surges in call volume were a wonderful opportunity to stretch and grow. We reaped huge rewards from a revenue perspective and I was moving the organization forward to regaining the millions of dollars previously lost. We were also on our way to showing a positive net contribution. I put together creative new programs that helped us with the growth, while at the same time ensuring top customer service satisfaction scores. That was the positive side. The negative side was that these large ramp-ups taxed everyone in the organization, from the recruiters to the human resources organization, from training to the quality department, and from operations to, of course, the IT department. Every level of leadership in my national organization was stretched thin as we geared up and moved through the ramp-ups. Sometimes we had more new leaders than veteran leaders in our virtual/work at home contact center. Everyone felt the strain.

When Jacob, our scheduling manager, called and told me we were being asked for more phone hours from our client, I just shook my head. How could I ask these people for more when they had already volunteered so many hours on top of the overtime hours that they were already scheduled to work? I had been asking for extra hours for months. Jacob asked me to do a video to request more volunteers for our rapidly expanding schedule. I hung up at the end of the call and got up out of my seat. I worked virtually from home as well, so I walked out onto my deck to think of something creative that I could say in my video.

I decided to enhance the "Dangle the Carrot" tool. With the concept of winning future business from our client, I built a foundation for "The Big Picture" and moved right into my enhanced version of the "Dangle the Carrot" tool from *The Leadership Toolbox*. I explained to my customer-facing front-line agents that when we earned future business from our client, we would promote over 75 people. I mentioned that we would need quality assurance people, supervisors, operations managers, and new trainers. We would also need over 100 people to help with new employees and training. My "carrots" were these 75-plus positions and over 100 helpers that we would need to assist new employees and conduct training roundtables as we expanded.

I believe in transparency, so I explained that new leaders in my organization would need a track record of stepping up and working more hours when we needed them. I explained the interview process and told them that one of the pre-interview considerations would be how many times they volunteered for extra hours on top of their already scheduled overtime. I went on to explain that a leader, even one without a formal leadership title, could influence other employees to jump in and help. I gave them real-life examples of how they could accomplish this and lead other employees to also volunteer for more phone hours. I also explained that we would be looking for specific examples in their interviews on how they encouraged others to help with a specific goal. My leaders, I went on, saw a need in the organization and filled it. They were proactive, and I was looking for more leaders with that kind of dedication and passion.

I thanked them and told them it was an honor to serve them as their leader. I also thanked them for believing in my leadership and for standing right beside me. I ended my video with my tag line that was a favorite of mine from my Zig Ziglar days: "See you at the top!" I edited the video and added music to it. It was posted on the home page of our intranet and then blasted out to the over 100 chat rooms that supported our work from home environment.

Less than 30 minutes later, my phone rang. It was Jacob, my scheduling manager. He chuckled and said, "I am looking at the live doc and can see employees signing up for the extra phone shifts. I knew if I called you and you did a video, they would step up." As the call volume continued to surge, we hit a record for additional hours that we staffed for our client, creating an all-time record for them. Our company executive team was thrilled with the additional revenue, which in turn increased our bottom line contribution.

The next day, I did another video. I used the "Everyone Has a Sign on Their Head That Says, 'Make Me Feel Important'" tool and I ended with "The Big Picture" tool, talking about our goal of winning new business from our client. I told them it felt great to lead a world-class organization with record top performance. I must admit that it was an emotional video for me. I knew the sacrifices they were making to take on more hours while providing excellent customer service.

Over the next few weeks, our client continued to ask for more phone hours. I was posting four to five videos a week to my organization. Each time, I told my organization the truth about what was happening. I spoke from my heart and explained how I felt about asking them for more hours when they were so tired. Then I used the "Everyone Has a Sign on Their Head That Says, 'Make Me Feel Important'" tool. I expressed how much I appreciated everything they had done. I acknowledged that they were tired and weary. We had added over 1,400 new agents over a 90-day period. I told my organization that our Fortune 500 client was shocked that we could hit such high customer service satisfaction scores, especially with so many new customer service representatives and newly promoted leaders with no previous management experience.

I read some emails from a few agents telling me how much they had learned from participating in this ramp-up season. I spoke directly to our new agents and thanked them for coming up to speed so quickly. I also thanked the supporting departments in the organization.

The months of massive amounts of overtime from my organization helped fill voids created when our client's other vendors couldn't meet their staffing requirements. During our client's largest international product launch in their history, we were credited many times on international vendor calls for "saving the day once again!" My leaders and I worked long hours. My agents pulled out all the stops, working 50, 60 and even 70 hours a week answering one call after another, with great performance. It was an emotional time for the organization, but in the end, we were successful.

Employees made a lot of overtime dollars and more performance bonuses. True to my word, we promoted more than 75 people, funded with additional business and new opportunities from our client. These newly promoted leaders did videos for us that we used strategically within the organization. They were testaments for working hard and achieving goals, which was the "carrot." We brought in record revenue for our organization, including monthly bonuses for our overall performance. Our company COO asked me how we turned things around, grew the organization, and increased our bottom line, all while repairing our reputation with our client. My reply was truthful. "It's the people. By leading them effectively and utilizing the right tools, we can accomplish anything."

Whether you are a front-line manager, middle manager, or senior leader, when you utilize multiple tools from *The Leadership Toolbox* as building blocks, you can see great results. Your teams will feel important and engaged in your business ("Everyone Has a Sign on Their Head That Says, 'Make Me Feel Important'"). Your teams will see the vision of where you are going ("The Big Picture") and what's in it for them ("Dangle the Carrot"). Your leadership bench will grow. Because employees are engaged, your company will "Save Money" on employee hiring because there will be less employee attrition. For a business process outsourcing company (BPO), you can generate "More Money" because the more people that show up for work, the more revenue increases. Happy employees mean better sales conversion, better customer service satisfaction scores, more productivity, and awesome new ideas for products and services. The company can make "More Money" in new customer acquisition and repeat business. You'll have happier and more engaged employees, happier customers that own your product or service, and increased revenue and bottom line contributions for your company. Everyone wins!

The "Dangle the Carrot" tool gives people another reason to show up and do their best. They get creative about how they can assist and serve your customers. This tool utilizes a core belief within our human nature. Think about how hard you work for things in your personal and business life. It's the "carrot" that keeps you moving forward. By utilizing this tool as a standalone tool or as a building block with one or more of the other tools in *The Leadership Toolbox*, you can multiply your efforts across your entire organization, achieving phenomenal results in a shorter period of time.

The People Know the Answer
Admit That Your People May Know More Than You Do

When I worked for Leon in his direct to consumer company, we marketed, sold, and shipped merchandise from our corporate headquarters in the Midwest. Shelia, a feisty woman with a passion for customer service, ran our shipping department. She prided herself on running a tight ship, making sure her department was clean and organized. The company was growing rapidly and, like every organization that is growing, we needed improved processes to keep up with the growth. As our company scaled operations, some of our top salespeople were dissatisfied with how long it took to ship merchandise out of the warehouse.

At that point in my career, I had no experience with shipping and receiving, so I went to Leon and asked him what I should do about the situation. He looked me in the eye and asked me what *I* was going to do about it. I told him I wasn't sure, which was why I was coming to him. I stood there waiting for him to say something, but he just smiled at me. I always knew when he smiled that something profound was going to come out of his mouth. He said he was going to tell me something that would change my career forever ("Dangle the Carrot"). He went on to say that he was going to tell me something that would help grow me as a leader, so that my organizations would always be the best ("The Big Picture").

Then he stepped back, looked at me and said, "The people know the answer."

I asked, "What the heck does that mean?" Leon was a good mentor and in his usual step-by-step mentoring approach, he started to ask me some questions.

"Who is the leader of the shipping room?" he asked.

"Shelia," I answered.

"Right," he said and then asked, "Who is the person who knows the most about the shipping of our products?"

"Shelia," I replied.

"You are right!" Leon declared. "Then if Shelia knows the most about the shipping and is the leader of the shipping department, why don't you ask her?"

"Because I am the manager and I should tell her what to do," I responded.

His expression didn't change as he replied, "But you just came in here to my office and told me that you didn't know what to do."

"But if I don't have all the answers, she will lose respect for me."

"No," Leon stated. "It will be just the opposite. She will have more respect for you if you ask for her opinion. After all, she is the subject matter expert on shipping here and she is the leader of that department. Trust me. Go and ask her." I agreed to ask her and left his office.

I walked into the shipping department and told Shelia that I appreciated her opinion ("Everyone Has a Sign on Their Head That Says, 'Make Me Feel Important'"). I then asked her what she thought could be done to streamline the shipping of the products. I explained to her that the salespeople felt they could get more referrals if the customers received their products faster. She turned around and went over to one of the shipping tables, bent down, and pulled out a rolled-up schematic plan of how she wanted to organize the shipping and receiving department. I was impressed by her initiative and complimented her ("Everyone Has a Sign on Their Head That Says, 'Make Me Feel Important'"). I told her I appreciated her readiness and to "go ahead and get it done." By the following week, all the new processes were in place. Products were sent out more quickly. The salespeople were happy, and sales continued to climb.

When I first go into an organization and ask leaders if they listen to their front-line employees, the answer is always "yes." They proudly tell me about their once-a-year employee engagement survey and employee suggestion box. They also assure me that they have an open-door policy. However, when

I ask their front-line employees how they feel when they speak up with their suggestions, they invariably tell me that their efforts were usually wasted because no one listened, and they ultimately stopped trying. That attitude of discouragement is contagious and spreads to others on the team. It can cause their work to suffer and productivity to go down. This is because other front-line employees have recognized the same challenges and also attempted to offer their opinions, only to be shot down too. I have seen legitimate ideas ignored because managers and leaders are too busy doing their own "check-off-the-box" lists to listen. Among other reasons, I have seen situations where leaders think they know more than their front-line employees.

In some cases, second-level managers have shot down front-line leaders' ideas. This is because when they went to the senior manager, their ideas were shot down too. I have even heard directors say the VP they report to has their own ideas on what they need to drive. So, again the level that is closer to the front lines is ignored because a leader believes they know more than the manager who reports to them. Yet, when metrics and timelines aren't met, some executives continuously demand corrections, while tying the hands of leaders and employees who have the answers!

I have found that this scenario often exists when there is no process for gathering information inside an organization or where there is no ebb and flow of ideas and discussion as part of the company culture. It seems that when we are task-driven, the overall strategy of moving the company forward ("The Big Picture") goes out the window. Thus, we perpetuate our own problems.

In a lot of companies, first and second-level leaders are organically grown from the front lines. This, in my opinion, is the number one reason why these leaders can struggle with the idea of going to the front lines. They believe that 1) they should know more than the people below them on the organizational chart and 2) it's their job as a manager or senior manager to tell people what to do. A barrier goes up, which could prevent the flow of ideas. This happens because in this type of scenario, these managers may have never been mentored or worked in an environment where there is an ebb and flow of ideas and discussions. Unmet challenges perpetuate, until they affect the bottom line and senior-level executives take notice. I believe that new leaders would accelerate learning with proper mentoring in the day-to-day trenches from an experienced leader.

If you are a leader and you believe ideas flow inside your organization, I would challenge you to ask your people what they think. If they agree, congratulations. If not, you might have an opportunity and "The People Know the Answer" tool in *The Leadership Toolbox* could be the answer to help your organization move ahead.

Case Study

A company hired my organization to help them win a yearly contract with their client. Our job was to qualify warm leads that were provided by our client and, if qualified, transfer those prospects to our client's sales team so they could continue the sales process and make the sale. Our client was on a six-month trial period to win a yearly contract and our job was to help them secure that contract.

About a month before the six-month trial period was over, our client's Vice President of Sales ordered me to have my team work on weekends to increase the qualified lead flow, so they could drive more sales conversion. At this point, the contract specifically said that we were to qualify leads for our client Monday through Friday from 9am to 9pm. The VP also informed me that he didn't think he should pay an additional fee for the extended hours of service he was asking me to provide. I told him that I would figure out a creative way to meet his goal, without any additional service costs to him and no additional labor costs to me.

I called an emergency management meeting in my office and explained the situation to my management and leadership teams. I received responses like: "Oh my gosh!" and "We can't do that!" They also declared, "The agents will never work weekends" and asked the question of all questions, "What if we lose the account? Will we have to lay people off?"

In an attempt to calm everyone down, I said, "Whoa, this isn't going to break us. Let's start some brainstorming."

One of my managers, Jessie, was extremely detail-orientated. With every idea the team came up with, he would quickly analyze and tell us the logical reason why that idea wouldn't work. While most leaders would see this as a negative, I valued Jessie's brain and his passion for speaking up. He always got me and the team thinking in a different way. We counted on his thoughts to help us uncover obstacles that could hinder our success. That day, he looked at me, shook his head and said, "This will never work, Vic."

Having used *The Leadership Toolbox* for years, I was confident that we could figure this out. I looked at my team and said, "We will just get the agents to decide how to change their schedules and how to work part of the weekends with no overtime ("The People Know the Answer")." Jessie looked at me, shook his head, and again said, "This is never gonna work, Vic."

I looked him square in the eyes and replied, "Watch us!"

I told my leadership and management team that I was going to meet with all the agents on this client account who were working that afternoon. I asked my leaders to stand in the back of the room while I spoke with the agents. They were instructed not to say a word in the meeting, unless one of the agents spoke to them. I told them that after I spoke with the agents, we, as the leadership and management teams, would "debrief." I asked them to take notes on how I handled the meeting and assured them that they were going to grow as leaders from this exercise ("Dangle the Carrot").

I could almost see the wheels of Jessie's brain turning. He asked, "How are you going to do this? How will you make them do this?"

"Jessie, I am not going to make them do anything," I explained. "They are going to come up with the plan to change their shifts and work part of the weekends, so we can help our client win their new yearly contract."

Later that afternoon, as the shifts changed, I rolled an 8-foot-long whiteboard right onto the operations floor and asked the agents to gather around. I noticed my leadership and management teams in the back of the room, exactly where I asked them to be. They were ready to take notes. I had invited the person who helped with the scheduling, as well as a couple of people from our IT department, to join us. I told the agents that we had a business challenge and I needed their help. I asked one of them to come up to the whiteboard and take some notes, so we could brainstorm. Then I explained the situation to them and what the client had "asked me" to do.

I told them that we were not going to charge our client an additional fee and that I couldn't pay overtime, because of our budget constraints. The agent taking notes on the whiteboard wrote down the challenge. Then I asked the agents to come up with some ideas so that we could handle the business goal. I looked up at Jessie. He stared straight at me. The agents just glanced at each other. No one said anything.

I went on, "Okay ladies and gentlemen, this is a real business challenge for us. We need to help our client get their contract ("The Big Picture")."

"This will mean more revenue and growth for our company ("Make Money")."

"When that happens there will be more leadership opportunities available in our leadership development program ("Dangle the Carrot")."

"I trust you to figure this out because you know this business and talk with prospects every day. I know if anyone can figure this challenge out, you can. I have all the faith in the world in you. I know you can do this ("Everyone Has a Sign on Their Head That Says, 'Make Me Feel Important'")."

I went on, "Who wants to make a suggestion first?"

A half an hour later, with my management team looking on, the agents had a list of strategies on the board. The agents asked Jessie for some reporting on when our high contact times were with our prospects. Jessie printed a report and gave it to one of them. They then asked him some technology questions, which he answered with ease.

It didn't take long for my front-line agents to come up with a plan, complete with a process for the team to sign up for shifts. They had determined how they could change their schedules and how they would figure out who could work on the weekends. People volunteered to sign up for split shifts, some even saying they could work three separate shifts in a day. I just kept nodding and smiling. The leadership and management teams just stared, and Jessie was in disbelief.

The agents had some homework to do because we needed to look at the schedule and figure out where we needed people and then plug the agents into those timeslots. When they asked if I would feed them, I replied, "I am sure the client will pay for pizza to feed all of us ("Save Money")."

Some of the management and leadership team members volunteered to bake goodies to keep energy high. Then one of the agents said the magic words every contact center member, at any level, loves to hear. "Why don't we have a pot luck each weekend during this push month?" Once I heard this, I knew we were going to hit a home run. Someone even asked if I would make my Italian aunt's famous meatball recipe. I thanked them for a great brainstorming session. I told them to work on the process in between calls and that the managers would be there to answer any questions. The agents passed around sheets so they could write down the hours they could work.

As they went back to their desks and logged in, my leadership and management teams crowded into my office. I quietly said, "The people know the answer." I talked about the tool and explained that being honest and forthright with the business challenge allowed the agents to come up with the same, or even better, solutions than we would have.

The leaders were excited, and Jessie looked mesmerized. I turned to him and asked, "Anything you'd like to add?"

"No thanks, Vic. That was amazing!"

"Yes, it was, Jessie," I said. "We have a great team and we're going to help our client get their yearly contract ("The Big Picture")."

After the leadership and management teams left my office, I picked up the phone to call the client. I explained that the team had figured out a way to help them get more leads so they could convert them to sales. He thanked me. I said, "I need you to feed them donuts in the morning and pizza for lunch and dinner. Will you do that?" He told me that wasn't a problem.

The team ultimately rose to the occasion. A creative schedule was produced and they pulled out all the stops. The leadership and management teams helped on the phones too, when necessary. We had pizza and baked goods for everyone. The agents decided to extend the potlucks to Friday, Saturday, and Sunday for the month as we raced towards the sales deadline!

The food was terrific. Everyone showed up for work and no one called in sick. If something came up, agents would just exchange shifts amongst themselves. I showed up on the weekends as well to support my team. The energy on the operations floor was amazing. The president of our company even came by and personally thanked the agents. They were so excited!

A month later, our client called to tell me that they won their yearly contract. This meant more business for us, as we continued to raise the bar in getting them more qualified leads, so they could convert those leads into sales. Some of the agents cried when they realized that we helped our client win their new contract. It was a real sense of pride for the organization and the whole company was buzzing with excitement.

This client's challenge and opportunity was a springboard to build more leaders and creative initiatives on my operations floor. Everyone learned "The People Know the Answer" tool. Our division continued to increase revenue and our bottom-line contribution. Moving forward, my leadership and management teams regularly went to the agents for input and were excited to hear their ideas. There was buy-in for initiatives because the agents were part of the brainstorming and then drove the initiatives themselves. In growing our division, we increased our hours and expanded our operations to seven days a week. Our employee attrition dropped to less than three percent annualized, which is unheard of for an outsourced contact center!

As leaders in any industry, we need to realize that our front-line employees have more real-time experience with our customer base than senior-level leaders. When we harness the creativity and expertise of these valuable employees, we can quickly figure out where our gaps are and get creative ideas for closing them. This saves time and money for the organization. When "The People Know the Answer" tool is utilized real time in a company, it becomes a habit. Glitches are identified quickly, and solutions come forward before problems show up in the metrics or on a P&L statement. Employees become more positive, more productive in their jobs, and more willing to solve problems themselves. They work together, with less employee issues because people feel valued. Employees are more engaged and happy at work.

"The People Know the Answer" tool creates new skill sets inside organizations, helping to develop formal leaders and a leadership mindset with the front-line employees. When we incorporate "The People Know the Answer" tool from *The Leadership Toolbox*, some employees will be very vocal. You can see the natural leadership come out of these people and you will observe other front-line employees follow these pseudo-leaders. Implementing this tool enables leadership mentoring programs to happen in real time, utilizing real business challenges and strategies to teach up-and-coming leaders. When you consistently use this tool, these new skills can be practiced over and over. Your leaders will create new productive habits, your leadership bench will deepen, and your teams will be energized. Confidence develops at all levels in your company and people will cultivate real respect for senior leadership.

If you want to gain traction in your organization, utilize "The People Know the Answer" tool. People come from different backgrounds and have varying thought processes, so getting everyone's input is important. Don't disregard the introverts. Sometimes those quiet, slow, and steady employees have great ideas. This is what I call authentic inclusion, and it's important to create an environment where this is possible throughout your organizations. Through authentic inclusion, you can mirror your customer base by utilizing "The People Know the Answer" tool from *The Leadership Toolbox* to come up with great ideas and accomplish phenomenal results.

The Mirror
Challenge Leaders to Accept Responsibility

I recently spoke to Mary, a Senior Vice President who runs global contact center operations for a multi-billion-dollar multinational company. Prepping for the discussion, I found that she had a master's degree from a top-tier university and had come to the organization after five years of working for a Fortune 200 company. During our video conference, I asked what challenges she was facing. Without hesitating, she replied, "Candidate sourcing, recruiting and training costs."

Next, I asked Mary about her employee attrition and absenteeism. I saw her throat gulp. Reluctantly she shared that the organization had over 175% annualized employee attrition and over 20% absenteeism. It usually costs a contact center anywhere from $2,500 to $5,000 to source, recruit, and train one new employee. It wasn't hard to do the math and see that her organization was bleeding money off their bottom line. I thanked her for being so honest and upfront with me and mentioned that a lot of organizations struggle with the very same issues. She nodded in agreement.

I asked Mary to tell me about her organization's culture. Her face lightened up and she said, "We have a great culture! People like working here." I wasn't surprised by her response. Business leaders are often mesmerized with their company culture and wear their definition of culture as a badge of honor. However, what they seldom recognize is that their own ego is tied to how they define that culture.

I looked square into the camera and said quietly and with sincerity, "With all due respect, Mary, with over 175% annualized attrition and 20% employee absenteeism, help me understand why your front-line agents are not showing up for work every day and why they are leaving your company if your culture is so great?" She just stared back at me, not knowing what to say. The silence was deafening. When she finally spoke, she started down a path of vigorously defending her company culture, even boasting that her company had won numerous awards. Yet, there was quantitative data proving that something was wrong. Had she even asked herself if there was a connection between the perceived culture and the over the top employee attrition and absenteeism?

Unfortunately, I see this almost everywhere I go. When I do the "deep-dive," I find that most executives believe that their organizational challenges can be fixed with improved performance training of front-line employees. Some executives blame the company's sourcing and recruiting organization or low compensation for problems with their front-line employee attrition and absenteeism. However, study after study demonstrates that money isn't the top motivator for staying with a company. Compensation is important, but it's not the main reason for high annualized employee attrition.

Our Reflection in the Mirror

"The Mirror" tool in *The Leadership Toolbox* is our reflection of how we see ourselves as leaders. Whatever we see becomes our truth. This tool can be very personal because it challenges each of us to look at ourselves and ask the question, "How do my leadership skills contribute to the success or failure of my organization?" Sometimes our egos can be like a pair of rose-colored glasses and alter what we see. It may be too painful to ask ourselves the tough question, "Are the gaps in my organization connected to the way I lead?" We fear that the answer may ultimately be "yes."

As leaders, we may have other fears as well, including:

- Someone finding out that we have made a mistake or overlooked something

- Losing our creditability within the company

- Losing our jobs

- Not getting promoted

- Not knowing how to fix problems inside our organizations

For any of these reasons and more, the answer for most leaders is to blame someone else or, worse yet, pretend there really isn't anything wrong. In these scenarios, leaders will continuously ignore the challenges within the organization until someone else notices some metric sliding and starts investigating.

Raising the Rate of Compensation by 25% and Still No Change in Employee Attrition

Another contact center organization I assisted, this one with 300 seats, had 215% annualized employee attrition when I started working with them. In other words, they had to hire over 600 people during their calendar year to ensure they could meet their staffing requirements of 300.

To get ready for a new product launch, this center's client requested they add an additional 300 head count to the existing 300, bringing the total headcount to 600 by the middle of the year. This meant that in order to add the additional 300 employees with this annualized employee attrition rate of 215%, they would have to hire well over 600 people (depending on the timing of the new hires) to meet their new service level requirements. That brought total hiring for the year to over 1,000, which is a conservative estimate.

After a quick calculation, I concluded that if they hired 1,000 people this year (the real number would end up being higher given the rapid escalation in work force required), at an average cost of $4,500 to source, recruit, hire, and train just one employee, that would bring the total cost of hiring to 4.5 million dollars. What hiring should have cost — given an assumed attrition rate of 25% — was approximately $2 million. This equated to a $2.5 million difference that was hitting their bottom line because they couldn't control employee turnover.

A member of the senior leadership team that managed this global organization firmly believed that attrition would be reduced significantly by a 25% increase in the employee base compensation. They implemented the change for the next seasonal surge, which occurred after they increased their employee base by 300 employees. Even with the increased salary, employee attrition did not go down. Instead, it stayed relatively consistent at 215%. They had increased their labor costs by 25% and were still losing over $3 million off their bottom line due to employee attrition.

The Blame Game

Leadership is constantly finding someone else to blame, whether it's the recruiting department, the training department, low compensation, or even a lack of employee coaching. I worked with one company that blamed their Fortune 500 client for their problems, because the client was too demanding. I've also been involved with companies where leaders acknowledge their problems, but in the next moment, stick their heads in the sand and pretend they don't see them. I worked with one CEO who refused to acknowledge the gaping hole in the technology assets within his company. It wasn't too long before he couldn't keep up with market conditions and was forced to close his business.

No leader is perfect, even the great ones we hear about. When you have challenges inside your organization, whether you are a CEO or a first-level supervisor, it's easy to blame other people in the organization for failures. If we blame someone else, we have less personal pain. We can even blame something else, like market conditions, lack of up-to-date technology, or budget constraints without seeing how we contributed to the challenge. There very well might be other conditions adding to the challenges in our organization, but we must always look at ourselves first. The ego is like a blanket that keeps us warm and cozy – and in total denial.

Our families, colleagues, and business network may play into our egos as well, so we don't have to face our challenges. These people can be our biggest proponents and help steer blame toward other people, conditions, or situations. As our cheerleaders, they can contribute to the nice, cozy, warm blanket of our egos, further magnifying the root of the problem.

"The Mirror" tool takes guts to use. It's the reflection we see in the mirror that points to us. It challenges us to look at ourselves first and ask ourselves the tough question, "How am I contributing to the gap we have in the organization?"

My dad first introduced me to this concept. He used to say, "Either you are part of the solution or you are part of the problem." I just refuse to play the victim role. I would much rather step up and get a situation fixed. If I am the reason my metrics, my gross revenue, expenses, or bottom line contribution are not where I want them to be, and I am not doing something I could be doing, I want to know. My attitude toward accepting responsibility in my organization is simple. If I am contributing to the challenge, then it's easy to fix because I am responsible for my attitude and my actions.

The entire organization can suffer when a leader isn't willing to use "The Mirror" tool and look at themselves first. If I'm not sure whether I am contributing to the situation that needs to be changed, I ask the people in my organization, including front-line employees, for their insights ("The People Know the Answer"). I simply pick up the phone and call them or send out a survey and then post the results. I can also utilize chat and email to communicate. You will be amazed what you learn when you aren't trying to skew the results. Hearing things that I don't want to hear can be difficult, but I feel I have a responsibility to my people, company, clients, and customers to keep my ego in check.

I know from experience that I can reach my goals more quickly if I surround myself with leaders who have no ego-driven desire to always be right. To drive change and get organizations quickly moving forward, there is no time for ego. Therefore, I surround myself with leaders who have a genuine quest for excellence and are willing to look at themselves before pointing the finger of blame. People respect leaders who behave in an open, receptive way. This kind of leadership makes employees more willing to show up for work and do their best.

Case Study

I worked with a CEO of a mid-size contact center organization. When I first met this CEO, he seemed very astute about his West coast company. After a more in-depth discussion, he confided in me that he just needed the right people at the top of his organization to be successful. We had several discussions over the following weeks where he told me of his constant turnover of operations managers, directors, human resources managers, and vice presidents. He thought he had been choosing the wrong people and they just couldn't adequately perform. I flew down to one of his contact centers to observe and spend time with him. He was sure I could tell him what he was doing wrong and help him "fix it."

On the first morning, I walked into the contact center to find many of the front-line agents out of their seats. The wall board at the end of the contact center floor noted that over 100 customers were waiting on hold to be serviced. On the left side of the contact center, there were two employees yelling, pushing, and shoving each other. This encounter had attracted a small group of employee onlookers.

I glanced across the rest of the contact center floor. There was a meeting room with floor to ceiling glass facing out onto the contact center on the right side. There was a meeting going on, with approximately 12 people sitting around the large conference table. I assumed that someone would come out to address the altercation, but no one moved from around the table. The receptionist out front heard the commotion and came in. We both stood at the end of the contact center. When I looked at her, she shrugged her shoulders and said, "That's a normal occurrence around here." I looked through the glass of the meeting room and waved in an attempt to get someone's attention. Someone waved back, and they continued their meeting.

Meanwhile, the fight on the left side of the room was getting louder. I was sure that the customers on the phone could hear the commotion. I walked over to the fighting duo and small crowd gathered around them. "Okay ladies and gentlemen," I said. "Let's break it up. We have customers waiting on the phone and we're letting them down." I turned to the small crowd of representatives that were watching these two customer service representatives push and shove each other and asked them to return to the phones to service the customers. The small crowd went back to the phones.

I asked the two representatives who had been arguing a few questions and learned that one of the agents had called the other agent a "lousy rep." I suggested it might be a good idea to go back to their seats and help the customers who were waiting for service. They went their separate ways, shaking their heads.

I glanced over at the meeting room. The people in the glass enclosed room could see me in plain sight. No one knew who I was and yet here I stood on the operations floor. I asked the receptionist where the CEO was. She said she didn't know. I asked her who was in the meeting room. She replied, "The managers."

A while later, the CEO came into the building and walked onto the operations floor. I saw him and walked over to greet him. He shook my hand and said he was glad to see me, then suggested we go into his office to talk.

Over the week that I was there, I realized that the CEO was not dealing with the reality of the situation. He had charts and graphs and a lot of data in his office, but had no clue how to turn the organization around. The clients whose phone calls this company answered were not happy with the results they received and were ready to cancel their contracts. I learned that he had hired nine senior-level people over the previous five years. He had terminated each of them within six to nine months.

I asked the CEO why he let each employee go. Each time he said they didn't understand his culture. I asked him to describe his culture. I had to make a conscious effort to not let my mouth hang open in disbelief as I listened to him. Finally, I asked him if the culture he described to me was the culture he actually had or the culture he wanted. He said he would have to think about it.

When I told him about the confrontation that had transpired on the operations floor, he just shook his head. He told me that he would look up some motivational videos on YouTube and have the employees watch them. This was not a 15-seat contact center. He had over 250 front-line agents in his organization in multiple locations. Every leader in the organization had been promoted from a front-line agent. There was no leadership development and mentoring going on, except for YouTube videos and leadership books that he would hand out. As call volume continued to increase, the organization's already taxed leadership skill set was continuously diluted because the promoted leaders didn't know how to lead. They were taught the basic management duties of reading reports, coaching, and doing attendance audits, but there was no one to mentor these new and existing leaders on how to motivate, inspire, and lead their teams to be top-performing rock stars. The entire organization was floundering and employee attrition was off the charts.

I talked with this CEO about "The Mirror" tool. He thought it was great, but his ego wouldn't let him see his contribution to the real problem. When I left there a week later, the CEO had a new game plan, but I knew in my heart that he had just wasted my consulting fee. He couldn't lead his organization. More importantly to note, he just couldn't see what was going on. To the average person off the street, it would have been obvious, but his ego would not allow him to recognize what was right in front of him.

"The Mirror" tool is not an easy tool to use. It takes a conscious effort to move our egos out of the way, so we can see what is really going on. How can we expect the leaders who report into us to honestly look at themselves and take responsibility for the decisions in their organizations, if we as leaders don't do the same?

Challenges within a company can cause huge amounts of money to be eroded off the bottom line and even negatively affect a brand within the market place. Unfortunately, these examples are not isolated. In my career, I have found these situations in small, midsize, and even multi-billion-dollar multinational companies.

Culture is important, and companies talk about it all the time. Unfortunately, if we don't utilize "The Mirror" tool and look honestly at the culture that we have created, either deliberately or accidently, the culture can allow gaps to exist within an organization, until they become gaping holes that bleed money off the bottom line. The bleeding won't stop until we change our behavior first, and as leaders, changing our behavior can take a lot of guts.

If you are having some challenges with "The Mirror" tool, then it's time to do a gut-check. Pull out the "The People Know the Answer" tool of *The Leadership Toolbox* and ask your teams where they think the challenges are within your company. After you get that information, pick up "The Mirror" tool again and have a real honest discussion with yourself. When we can put our egos in check and utilize "The Mirror" tool, we take a big step in authentically moving our organizations forward to build a chain reaction of success.

Third-Party Story
Get Your Point Across Faster and Inspire Momentum

As leaders, we must walk a fine line when giving employees instructions. If we just bark orders or send memos telling employees what they need to do, we run the risk of adversely affecting people within our organization – even if they agree with what needs to be done. So, how do we communicate with our employees in a way that will have a positive impact, get them to want to do something different, and get the desired result?

Think about the last time you went and listened to a keynote speaker. What sticks out most in your mind from what you heard? It's usually the stories that the speaker told. Stories can make you feel inspired, motivated, validated, fearful, and apprehensive. They can also encourage you to think about something you hadn't considered before. We remember these stories because they resonate with something that is important to us.

I call this strategy the "Third-Party Story" tool and I have illustrated it throughout *The Leadership Toolbox* with case studies. I have found that utilizing stories when you talk with a colleague, employee, or leader can be the catalyst for helping them to remember the point you are trying to make. In fact, people might forget the stats or specific numbers and dates that you have given them, but they will tend to remember a story that impacts them.

I have taught this tool to both customer-facing employees and leadership. It's a great resource that can make an impression on your employees, help you emphasize a point in a meeting, and have an impact when presenting an idea to your boss or an executive. When we talk with someone about an issue they perceive as negative, they may feel we are attacking them. So, they put a wall up around themselves to avoid feelings of discomfort. Once the wall goes up, the person is no longer able to hear you or comprehend the point you are trying to discuss. We all know what that feels like. This tool can help protect the ego of the person you are talking with because the emphasis is on the person in the story and not on the listener.

Telling impactful stories takes practice and a certain methodology. The stories can be as little as 15 seconds or can go on for five minutes or more, depending on the situation. As you start to develop your "Third-Party Story" telling skills, I suggest you start with shorter narratives while you are learning the methodology.

Often, when I first teach this tool, people are concerned that they don't have stories to tell. However, if you are like most people, you have likely witnessed a great amount of "story material" in your professional life. As a leader, you have consistently witnessed trends in employee attitudes, personalities, and performance. For example, you have probably coached multiple employees who have been late for work, not finished projects on time, or ignored company processes. You have talked with employees who used all their PTO in quarter one and wanted more time off. You have seen people react poorly when passed over for promotions or become angry when terminated from their position. As a leader, you have also seen employees turn around their performances, work hard to get promotions, and come up with brilliant ideas. All of these scenarios can be included in your own "Third-Party Story" library.

Over the years, this tool has become a habit for me. I tell stories when I talk with prospective clients, current customers and clients, employees, and executives within a company. In my personal life, I tell third-party stories to my friends, my gardener, my hair stylist, and my adult children. Stories are effective for quickly illustrating a point in a way that people will remember.

If you are a new leader or future leader, please don't worry. You can use someone else's stories and leave out their names. Here are some examples:

- "A friend of mine who manages an organization mentioned to me..."

- "A colleague told me about a client who..."

- "A while back, one of my employees told me…"

- "I was talking with someone in our industry and they told me a story about…"

- "A colleague of mine read this article in a magazine that talked about …"

It doesn't matter to the listener if the story happened to you personally or to someone else you know. They will remember the story and it will help them remember the point you made during the discussion.

To discuss the "Third-Party Story" tool, I will first talk about the simple methodology of the story and break down the three key components of the tool. Second, I will give you some specific examples and third, I will teach you how to start your own "Third-Party Story" library.

Third-Party Stories Are Memorable!

I led a large 2,000 employee national technical support organization where the entire operations team, including training, nesting, and quality assurance teams, worked remotely from their homes. I created three to five videos a week, utilizing stories to illustrate specific points I was making to drive strategy, new initiatives, and team performance.

Since I also worked virtually, I could travel anywhere and still work, so I decided to travel across the United States for a year with my 100-pound labradoodle, Webster. During this fantastic experience, I met a lot of my virtual/work from home employees at Starbucks along the freeways and highways, as well as in hotel meeting rooms. During our discussions, they would bring up the videos and tell me that they could relate to Susie trying to get promoted; Bob struggling when he first started with the company; or Ted feeling overwhelmed when he became a new manager. They remembered each of these stories because they emotionally connected with the situation. The "Third-Party Story" made such a lasting impression on them that they could relate the story back to me during our discussions.

Now, let's break the "Third-Party Story" tool down into three simple components: the *situation,* which illustrates the issue you want to address, the *action* that was taken in response to the situation, and the *result* of the action.

First Component - The *Situation* of the "Third-Party Story" Tool

How you approach a "Third-Party Story" situation depends on who you are talking to and what you are trying to accomplish. If the person or group of people you are talking with has a struggle or challenge, you would offer a story that involves the same struggle or challenge. Some examples include employee absenteeism, missing a revenue goal, the fear of being laid off, or anxiety about a promotion.

If the person or group of people is moving down the road toward the goal, then present the story in a positive light, with the assumption that they will ultimately reach their goal. The "Third-Party Story" tool will psychologically motivate them, setting them up for a positive end result. They will also assume that you believe they are going to accomplish the goal. Examples of this type of story might be:

- Someone working their way up to get a promotion
- The organization winning a new line of business
- A project coming in on time
- Meeting a recruiting goal
- Decreasing shipping times

Another use of the "Third-Party Story" tool involves situations where things are going well, but you see a huge obstacle ahead that you want to warn the listener about. Instead of saying, "Hey, you are approaching a big speed bump. The PO process in this company takes forever. I'm just warning you," you could tell a story of a time when the procurement team was going to hit a speed bump and how they got in front of the potential challenge, so it didn't derail the desired end result. You're basically telling them the same thing, but psychologically, you will evoke a different response in them. The more positive and inspirational you can be as a leader or colleague, the more people will listen and follow you. You can be an influencer instead of the negative person in the room.

Second Component - The *Action* Part of the "Third-Party Story" Tool

The action part of the "Third-Party Story" tool involves the specific actions that were taken to address the situation. The action will help the listener in solving their challenge or struggle without telling them what to do. It can also reinforce what they are currently doing, so that you are validating their actions while still offering suggestions for improved performance.

Third Component - The *Result* Part of the "Third-Party Story" Tool

The result part of the "Third-Party Story" tool in *The Leadership Toolbox*, should articulate the result you are trying to convey to the listener. We want to inspire the listener to take action, so the result needs to be relatable in order for the story to be impactful.

The result can be concise, or you can also add descriptive words to illustrate how the people in the story felt. This can be another way to get your listener emotionally connected to the result. The goal is to create a connection between the listener and the story in that moment. We also want the story to have a lasting impact. The more the listener remembers, the more they can reference the story, including the specific action they can take and the potential results they can accomplish. As they move towards their goal and start seeing positive results, their confidence will grow.

To best illustrate the components of the "Third-Party Story" tool, I am going to use four real-world examples. For each example, I will demonstrate how to build a compelling and memorable "Third-Party Story."

Example of a "Third-Party Story" Addressing a Struggle or Challenge

The Situation

"A while back, one of my managers, Sue, had an employee who was always late for work."

Now, let's add some descriptive words to this story. Adding descriptive words to the situation of the "Third-Party Story" tool can pull the listeners in closer and make your story even more interesting and memorable. By using descriptive words to illustrate how the subject of your story felt, you can help your listener become emotionally connected right from the beginning.

> "Sue was beside herself with frustration. She felt she had tried everything possible to get Kathryn, one of her employees, to come to work on time. She was at her wit's end."

The Action

You can make the action part of the "Third-Party Story" tool as long or as short as you like. If you go for the short version, your listener may ask questions, which shows that they are emotionally involved in what you are saying.

> "So, Sue sat Kathryn down and found out what she aspired to achieve in her career. Sue listened to everything that Kathryn said and came up with a game plan to help her move toward that goal. Sue promised that she would set up a meeting with managers from the two departments Kathryn was interested in joining.

> Sue also shared her concerns about Kathryn not showing up for work on time, but offered to recommend Kathryn for another position, if she showed up to work on time in her current job. Even if Kathryn did not show up on time, she would keep her word and get those discussions set up. However, she knew that the department manager would probably ask her about Kathryn's attendance and performance. She told Kathryn that she would have to tell the truth."

The Result

The result is the positive ending to the story. We want the listener or group of people to emotionally connect with the result and believe that they can have the same type of outcome in their specific situation. This part of the "Third-Party Story" tool in *The Leadership Toolbox* should get the listener excited and inspired to act.

> "Sue and Kathryn worked out a slight schedule change and Kathryn committed to be on time for a month before Sue would schedule the

meetings with the two department heads. In the end, each kept their word and Sue spoke to the two department heads. They were happy to set up a discussion time with Kathryn.

Six months later, Kathryn moved to another department with a small promotion. It was a win-win situation. Others saw Kathryn come to work on time, and when she was promoted into another department, it inspired everyone. Sue and the other department heads came up with a cross-training program so that people could get experience in other departments when they had acceptable attendance. They even asked Kathryn to help with the program."

Here is another example of a "Third-Party Story" addressing a struggle or challenge:

The Situation

"One of my sales managers, Steve, hadn't met the team quota for three consecutive quarters and was worried he was going to lose his job and be replaced."

With the addition of descriptive words:

"He seemed to be doing the same thing, expecting different sales results. When I asked him what his thoughts were, he told me that he felt the sales quota was just too high and unrealistic. He seemed to be frustrated and emotionally withdrawn from his team."

The Action

"When Steve stepped back and looked at his sales game plan, he realized that he had been on autopilot for some time, expecting different results. He sat down with his team and apologized for letting them down. Then, he asked for their help. It turned out that the team was ready with a new game plan and just waiting for him to ask. They believed the new plan could get them closer to the goal.

Steve approved the new plan, which included some 'quick hits' to get the ball moving forward again. Steve set up a meeting with his boss to lay out the plan. He asked the team to do the actual presenting, since they had all been part of the planning."

The Result

"The meeting with Steve's boss was a huge success! He opened the meeting by talking about the gaps in the sales department and giving his team credit for pulling a plan together. When the team got done presenting the plan, not only was the boss impressed, but he also agreed to give Steve extra marketing funds to help get the job done.

As people were leaving the room, the boss stopped Steve and complimented him on his leadership. Steve gave the credit to the team. They were just a tad shy on hitting the sales quota that quarter, but they hit it every quarter after that. Steve is still with the company and when his boss took another job in Florida, Steve took his place as the VP."

Examples of a "Third-Party Story" Assuming That a Goal Is Going to Be Accomplished

The Situation

"I remember when one of my friends, Bethany, was working toward a promotion in a great company."

The addition of descriptive words deepens the story and starts the listener down the path of confidence that the challenge will be met once a plan is in place and executed. For assumptive stories, the descriptive words assume that victory will be the end result.

"She was one of the most confident people I have ever seen. Even in the face of adversity, she could motivate herself by serving others. Bethany was an inspiration for all of us."

The Action

"When I watched Bethany, I noticed that she greeted everyone at the beginning of the shift and said something positive to them. She always kept the team's goals in front of them. Even though she wasn't the leader, she acted as if she were. No one minded, because she had each person's best interest at heart and she always gave the team credit for their accomplishments. Bethany had the ability to troubleshoot any situation and find a solution. People really respected her."

The Result

"A senior vice president noticed Bethany in a meeting and asked Bethany's boss about her. Her boss just raved about Bethany's leadership skill set, even though she had no formal title.

A few months later, the Senior Vice President was putting together a task force for a customer service initiative and wanted the task force to have people from every department. She specifically wanted Bethany to join the team. As usual, Bethany's leadership skills shined through and within just a few months, she was promoted to a formal management position. Everyone on the team was excited for Bethany because they knew she deserved it."

Now, let's look at one more example of a "Third-Party Story" that addresses the positive and assumes that a goal will be met.

The Situation

"Mark puts together great recruiting plans to handle huge product launches. He's been in the business for years and is a recruiting genius."

With the addition of descriptive words:

"Failing is never an option for Mark. He has a way of harnessing all the great talent in the group to come up with innovative and 'out-of-the box' recruiting plans. His teams always hit their target."

The Action

"Mark's plan was to divide us into small teams and have each of us identify any gaps that were in last year's holiday recruitment season. Once we did that, each team came up with a stop gap for each of those challenges. Third, we all got together and prioritized the ideas, finalized our game plan, and executed it. If needed, the plan was tweaked as we went along."

The Result

> "It was a huge success! We even had extra people in the recruiting pipeline, so we were ready for anything. Mark and the team saved the day. I'll never worry about recruiting for a major launch again."

Moving Forward with the "Third-Party Story" Tool

When moving forward with the "Third-Party Story" tool in *The Leadership Toolbox*, there are a few other details you should consider. If you are in a face-to-face situation with the listener or a team, you want to make sure your body language evokes agreement. For example, crossing your arms across your chest can come off as a defensive action. Nodding slightly every five or so seconds as you are telling your story encourages your listener to connect with what you are saying. Also, eye contact is very important. It shows that you are acknowledging your audience and that they have your undivided attention.

Conveying stories on the phone can be more challenging because you can't see the reaction of the listener, nor can they see your positive body language as you are speaking. Practice using different tones and pauses in your voice as you speak to keep the listener's attention. It is also useful to ask a question at the end of your story to further pull in your audience. Questions like "Does that make sense?" and "What are your thoughts about that?" encourage the listener to become an active participant in the story.

Creating a "Third-Party Story" Library

In my opinion, the best way to initially prepare your "Third-Party Story" library is to make a list of the situations you come across every day in whatever industry or vertical you are in. As a leader, you should be able to come up with five to ten situations you encounter on a daily or weekly basis. Think about the challenges you have within your own company, division, department, or team. Once you start your list of situations, you can then add the actions and the results as bullet points. Once you have your bullet points, you can go back and write out the details. Write the stories to sound like how you speak, then practice reading them out loud, so they will sound more natural.

Advance Your Career by Utilizing the "Third-Party Story" Tool

During my years working in various leadership roles, I have taught the "Third-Party Story" tool as part of an overall strategy to help people get promoted in my expanding organizations. The positive results communicated in the stories have inspired employees to hit their own performance metrics and accomplish their goals. Utilizing the "Third-Party Story" tool in *The Leadership Toolbox* has helped leaders and front-line employees showcase their achievements and achieve positive results in their interviews. I have seen huge success with this tool in driving overall performance within an organization. It helps employees focus on what they can contribute to the overall success of the business and work towards the results illustrated in the stories in an effort to be promoted.

As with all the tools in *The Leadership Toolbox*, this tool is simple to understand, relatively easy to learn, and it works. To articulate the point you are trying to make, as you drive an idea or initiative, become a master storyteller. By utilizing the "Third-Party Story" tool consistently, you will become proficient and gain a valuable habit that will help you lead your people, get them emotionally engaged, and drive results. Challenge yourself to use a story once or twice a day when talking with an employee or in a meeting. You can inspire and motivate the people in your organizations, building a chain reaction of success, and maybe even get that promotion yourself!

Meet Them Where They Are
Help Employees with Great Potential to Get out of Their Own Way

The first seven tools in *The Leadership Toolbox* demonstrate how understanding basic human behavior helps us approach our employees in a way that contributes to their success.

Promoting the right people into the right positions within an organization is like a game of chess, with many moving pieces and strategies. However, in business, these "pieces" are human beings with feelings and emotions. As a company grows, there is a pressing need to move people into positions with more responsibility, but we also want to ensure that they are placed into positions that match their skill sets. As we all know, timing is everything within the business world. Let's consider some common leadership questions:

- How do you get people to willingly follow you, so you can meet your goals inside your company?

- How do you help your employees find the right fit inside your company, where they feel challenged and love coming to work?

- How do you know what the right position is for an employee within your organization, especially when they aren't sure either?

- How do you get your people to stretch so they can grow and be ready for the next step in their career?

- How do you know when employees are ready for promotion, so you can set them up for success?

Throughout my career, I have consistently seen companies promote people before they are ready. While we want an employee's new position to challenge them, if the stretch is too big, we set them up for emotional disappointments. When too many leaders are promoted before they are ready, the management skill set can become diluted as a whole. This sets up an organization for all kinds of challenges and eroding key performance indicators. We can see various metrics affected, including loss of employee productivity, reduction in sales conversion, plummeting customer satisfaction scores, runaway expenses, more accidents in the plant or warehouse, and higher employee attrition. We may start seeing gossip affect productivity inside the organization, as employees talk about their new leader's struggles. Deadlines aren't met, which can reduce revenue, and people can lose faith in the leadership of the company.

When organizations scale quickly, either due to growth or seasonal surges, the wrong leadership can be the difference between success and failure. It can erode the organization's culture and dramatically affect revenue streams, costs, and ultimately net profit.

One way to help employees and leaders down the development path is to grab *The Leadership Toolbox* and find the "Meet Them Where They Are" tool. Each employee has different skill sets, emotions, life experiences, and goals. This means that they are at a place in their development that is unique to them. Leadership development programs, coaching, and individual mentoring should not be one size fits all. By understanding where our employees are emotionally and skill-set wise, we can "Meet Them Where They Are" and help them be more successful. This is absolutely critical in moving an organization forward. The best training is first-hand experience, which differs from the typical performance management plans often utilized by managers and approved by human resource departments.

While formal performance plans are important, they are seldom sufficient at moving the organization forward or turning things around if there are operational challenges. Formal performance plans often list the skills, activities, classes, or projects the employee needs to accomplish. Yet, even when these tasks are completed, employees may not be ready to successfully take on more responsibilities within the organization. I believe that to get employees to the next level, the manager needs to have a stake in their success and participate in it. Not only does the manager need to understand where employees are in their skill sets, but they also need to understand what emotionally drives them towards success.

For the "Meet Them Where They Are" tool in *The Leadership Toolbox*, I will be providing two case studies. The first will showcase an example of meeting an employee where they are with their skill set and the second will exemplify meeting an employee where they are emotionally.

Case Study

I took a position to help expand a work at home contact center workforce. The client, a large Fortune 500 company, had huge annual holiday ramp ups and international product launches that taxed the entire organization. One of the most significant areas of concern was making sure that the supervisor and assistant manager level leaders were ready to be promoted so they could hit the ground running and be successful. Since we had hundreds of new customer-facing agents starting every other week, this organization was feeling the pressure.

Inside this work at home environment's organizational structure, they had a team of 20 customer-facing agents reporting to one supervisor and five supervisors reporting to one assistant manager. There were a few challenges that I needed to address:

- The assistant manager's job was to manage through another layer of leadership – the supervisor level. These assistant managers were promoted because they were great supervisors, not because they had shown the skill set necessary to be successful in the assistant manager position. Though they already knew how to supervise front-line agents, these assistant managers didn't know how to duplicate themselves by training and mentoring a front-line leader to do a great job, just as they had once done in that position. Because the organization was growing so fast, this diluted skill set within the assistant management positions caused all kinds of issues, including frustration of newly promoted supervisors and the customer-facing agents they served.

- Five supervisors, each with 20 customer-facing agents on their teams (100 total agents), were too much for an assistant manager to handle, largely due to the fact that in their previous positions, they only managed 20 customer-facing agents and no additional managers. The jump in skill set to their new positions was too wide, and these assistant managers were overwhelmed. We saw failure after failure, even though these newly appointed leaders tried their best.

- The newly promoted front-line supervisors, who reported to the assistant managers, were being trained on how to run reports, how to check quality scores, how to coach, and how to learn new systems. Yet, they weren't being taught how to inspire and motivate an agent to serve the customers. These new supervisors also weren't being trained to identify and diffuse potential issues before they became major problems. Instead, the company was just perpetuating the diluted skill set of the assistant manager level.

These three challenges caused us significant pain, including employee productivity, employee absenteeism, and eroding customer service satisfaction scores. All of this equated to lost revenue and lost net contribution. I needed to evaluate the current team and organizational structure. I looked at their results, their management style, and how they held their meetings. I also considered how they conducted performance management and oriented themselves toward strategic and tactical initiatives. I looked at these leaders' work ethic, how they approached people, and their level of professional maturity.

Professional maturity (not age) is critical in leadership. You can utilize training classes and company universities, but in my opinion, professional maturity takes time to cultivate. Leaders must lead by example, so people have someone to emulate. At this point, the assistant managers were frustrated, the supervisors were just trying to make it through their day, and the front-line agents were not engaged. The business units were struggling to meet their metrics, which in turn meant the customers were frustrated and not getting their issues resolved. Every day brought new challenges on top of the mounting list from the previous day.

Delia, one of our assistant managers, was adored by everyone. Once people were on one of Delia's five teams, they never wanted to leave her. In fact, some of her team members would cry if we asked them to move teams for any reason. Delia was like a "mother hen" and took a great deal of care and personal pride in her business unit performance. Even with Delia's business unit culture and passion, her teams couldn't make the performance metrics she believed they should be making.

I decided to try an experiment and asked Delia to help me by only leading two teams in her business unit, instead of five teams. She did a great job with two teams, so in a couple of months, we added another one. However, her customer service satisfaction scores (CSATs) and other metrics declined under her management of three teams.

I had my business analyst look at the numbers and trends in her three teams. He suggested that we take one of those teams away and give her a different third team, with more top-performing, customer-facing agents on it. After a month, we realized that, even with the top-performing agents, Delia's three teams still were not meeting the CSATs we believed they could. Delia felt frustrated.

In her previous position as a supervisor, Delia was great at turning around customer-facing agents. She could take nonperforming agents who were at 50% to 60% CSATs and move them to 90% CSATs in a couple of weeks. Now that she was an assistant manager, she struggled with having the same impact on nonperforming agents, particularly when given three teams instead of two. For some reason, she struggled with adequate management of the agents when working through the three team supervisors. I talked with Delia and suggested that we once again take one of the top-performing teams away temporarily and leave the two existing teams with her. She agreed.

Within a couple of weeks, the two teams were in top-performing status. We congratulated Delia and gave the same third team back to her. It was still a top-performing team but had been managed for those couple of weeks by another leader. The team members were ecstatic to be back with Delia.

In a few short weeks, we started seeing Delia's business unit slipping in the team standings again. I called my business analyst and asked him to do some additional analysis. After looking at the numbers, he noted that some of Delia's nonperforming agents had previously been among the top-performing agents. The analysis showed that the teams were not the problem – it was Delia. She just couldn't handle three teams. Of course, the fix seemed easy. Just give everyone two teams instead of five to solve our assistant manager skill set issue and keep the customer service satisfaction scores up. I laughed along with everyone else on the conference call when that suggestion was made, because it clearly wasn't an option. That type of change would affect our labor costs and decrease our net profit. It simply was not a viable solution.

We consistently kept Delia in the loop during all of this. She was heartsick at the thought of failing. Both Delia and I were tea drinkers, so I asked her to set aside some time in the evening for virtual tea together. I said to her, "Let's just talk things through."

I met with Delia that evening and we had tea "together" on the phone. I explained, based on her metrics, that I thought three teams were too much for her to manage. I went on to explain that I felt I hadn't "met her where she was" because no matter what I had tried, the results weren't there. I didn't know what to do.

She said passionately, "I can't be defeated. Let me try another month before you take the third team away." I paused because I knew that I couldn't put the customer experience at risk. Instead, I offered to have another top assistant manager work with her. She agreed, but by the end of the next month, it was obvious that managing three teams just was not a good fit for Delia.

I called Delia and asked for another "tea time." I went back to *The Leadership Toolbox* and pulled out "The People Know the Answer" tool. That evening, I asked her, other than managing the teams, what three things she loved to do. Her answer threw me for a loop because it involved the hardest tracking metrics in our virtual contact center environment. It was the piece that kept me up late into the evening worrying – tracking employee attendance within our current systems. Some of our existing attendance reporting wasn't accurate. We used multiple reports that didn't always come up with the same numbers. We were in a virtual/work from home environment, so we couldn't see people sitting at their desks in a physical location. We had technology, but it was too time consuming and ineffective. Delia said she had lots of ideas, and I could feel her passion through the telephone.

When one of your top employees who is trustworthy, smart, has a great work ethic, and people love to work with her volunteers for your number one headache, it isn't hard to say yes. I told her, "Go for it, Delia!" She did just that, managing two teams and the attendance calculation process. She did a wonderful job and transformed our processes. We were also able to centralize additional procedures under Delia's leadership, which meant that the entire supervisor base within our national work at home contact center had more time to coach and develop their customer-facing agents. They were ultimately able to handle more teams, while meeting or beating our CSAT goals.

Every time Delia saw a process challenge that affected the organization, she would look at it, improve the process, and centralize it if it made business sense. In the end, I "met her where she was." As the organization grew, Delia recruited team members and her department became the "go to" team inside the organization. She more than paid for herself and her team through the process she developed and cost savings she created for the organization.

"Meet People Where They Are" is an extremely useful tool. As leaders, we can emotionally connect and help move an employee forward, so that we not only support the organizational initiatives, but we also help individual employees increase their skill set, which makes them feel good about themselves and their abilities. This is a critical component to the success of this tool. When people feel management cares enough to "meet them where they are," they become eager to learn and to perform. It's a win-win situation.

If you can't figure out how to determine where an employee is, use "The People Know the Answer" tool. Delia willingly gave me the information I needed to "meet her where she was." Her leadership skill set grew, and she hit a home run out of the park for the entire organization.

While this case study was about "Meeting People Where They Are" based on an employee's *skill sets*, let's look at a case study that illustrates utilizing this same tool when based on the *emotions* of an employee.

Case Study

Early in my career, I went to work for a midsized business process outsourcing company (BPO) that wasn't profitable. By the time I reached three months of tenure, we had built a training department, reduced employee absenteeism by 50%, and slashed attrition from 90% annualized to under 10% annualized. I developed new sales training and coaching programs, skyrocketing our top clients' sales conversion by 50%, 100%, and on some accounts by even 200%. We had utilized the tools in *The Leadership Toolbox* to create a solid culture and creative growth strategies.

We had numerous nice people who worked hard and helped us grow, but I was looking for A+ players to move into leadership. As I interacted with employees, I continuously noticed Tammy, one of our customer service representatives. It seemed that, whenever I turned around, I saw Tammy surrounded by people, even if they were not on her team. She had great people skills, was process-driven, and was quick to notice gaps in operational processes. The downside to Tammy's performance was that she was always late for work. When I say always late for work, I mean always – as in every day.

I knew that Tammy's manager had talked with her many times about her absenteeism. One afternoon, I asked her manager to come into my office. I asked the usual questions. Was there performance documentation? Had she talked with her about her tardiness? Did she offer Tammy a schedule change? She answered yes to each question.

Then I said, "If you don't mind, I'd like to talk with Tammy about her attendance."

Her manager smiled and said, "Go for it!"

So, the next day I saw Tammy coming down the hall toward the break room and asked her to stop by my office before she left that afternoon. When Tammy arrived, I walked to the other side of the desk, so I could sit down next to her. I explained that I thought she was a dynamic leader, to which she quickly responded, "I am not a leader."

I replied, "Well, you don't have to have an official title to be a leader." I went through my list of what I had seen her accomplish with her attitude, charismatic personality, ability to help people, identification of gaps, and ability to come up with new creative processes. She was a real consensus-builder with every department in the company, and I mentioned how it was so obvious to me that everyone loved working with her ("Everyone Has a Sign on Their Head That Says 'Make Me Feel Important'").

I asked her why she wasn't a manager. She replied, "I have an attendance problem. I just can't get here on time." When I asked her why, she looked at me and shrugged her shoulders, saying, "I don't know why."

I leaned forward and quietly said, "We need people like you in leadership positions to keep up with our company growth. You have a bright future in front of you. There is more money in leadership and you can help more people. Don't you want to move into management?" She responded that she did.

I went on to explain that leaders needed to lead by example and that her attendance stood in her way. Tammy's poor attendance behavior was also a risk to the organization because we needed to be consistent in our attendance processes and policies.

I asked what I could do to help with her attendance. She said that Laura, her team leader, had asked her the same question and that she had been given multiple schedule changes. Yet, she was still consistently late. I went on to tell her what I expected, what her future held for her, and that I was depending on her ("Dangling the Carrot"). We ended the discussion smiling at each other, especially when she said, "I'll do it!"

The next day she was late for work. So much potential and she was standing in her own way.

That night, Tammy was on my mind. Why did she go out of her way for others and not for herself? As I thought through all of this, I came up with all sorts of possible answers. After more than an hour, I realized that I should just ask Tammy ("The People Know the Answer").

The next day, I asked Tammy to come into my office before she went home. This time, I concentrated on all the positive things she had done and walked through them again with her ("Everyone Has a Sign on Their Head That Says, 'Make Me Feel Important'"). I talked with her again about her ability to connect with people, build relationships, and help them with their duties, regardless of what department they worked in. I asked her, "How does that make you feel when you help them?" She explained that it made her feel really good and that she felt important because her skills could assist them.

By her own admission, Tammy helped others because it made her feel important and useful. She loved it when people gave her positive feedback. This in turn made her feel good about herself.

We had a nice discussion, and I didn't mention her absenteeism. In the end, I walked her to the door and she hugged me as we said goodbye.

As I drove home that evening, I thought about my discussion with Tammy. I needed to come up with a plan to "meet her where she was." It needed to fit where she was emotionally and feed into her need to receive positive attention from people she worked with. I thought my concept was solid, but still was not exactly sure what to do. Tammy had the characteristics of a great leader, and I knew that helping her create a new habit would change her career and probably her life.

The next morning, I still didn't have a game plan. When I got to the office, I walked around and greeted employees in each wing and various departments of the contact center. When I got to Tammy's area, everyone in her pod of cubes thought I was coming to call her on the carpet for being late yet again. Tammy stood up and immediately started to make an excuse for being late. I quietly told her, "I'm not listening to any of this today," and motioned for her to follow me.

We walked into my office and I shut the door. She opened her mouth and started to explain again why she was late. I quietly said, "Stop." She looked at me. I said to her, "I am not having the conversation again with you about your absenteeism." I stepped back, looked her straight in the eyes, and said, "If you show up on time for 30 days in a row, I will dance on a table in the middle of each wing of the contact center. Oh, and by the way, I am a lousy dancer. But I'll do something that is so difficult for me, because I'm asking you to do the same. The clock starts tomorrow morning."

I walked over to my office door and opened it. She walked out, turned around, and said, "Really?"

I replied, "Yes really. I better start taking a dance lesson or two, just in case you meet my challenge." I smiled and said, "Have a great day." I walked back to my desk, leaving the door open. When I sat down and looked up, she was smiling at me.

As I thought about it, I realized that the easy part was done. Now, I needed to come up with a way to get her the emotional attention she craved. I needed to do something that would get her excited enough to tell everyone about the challenge. I knew if everyone got involved and gave her attention, she would probably rise to the occasion. It was at least worth a shot.

After lunch, I took a stack of 8-1/2 x 11-inch pieces of paper and put a number on each of them with a black marker. I started with "1" on the first piece of paper, then put a big "2" on the next piece, followed by a "3" on the third piece. I continued until I had labeled them up to the number "30." Next, I punched a hole in the two top corners of each sheet. I then took two small nails and a hammer from my credenza drawer and walked into the hallway right outside of my office. I hammered the two small nails into the wall, so they would line up with the holes in the paper, right at eye level. Then, I loaded the sheets of paper with the numbers onto the nails, starting with the "1" page on the bottom of the stack and ending with the "30" page on the top of the stack.

As Tammy left for the day, she noticed the stack of pages with the numbers on the wall outside my office. When I saw her, I got up and walked out into the hallway. We stood outside my office door and chatted. I waited for her to ask me about the sheet with the "30" on it. I knew she wouldn't be able to resist.

"Vic, what is this for?" she asked as she pointed toward the stack of papers hung on the two small nails.

"Oh…that's for you," I replied.

"What do you mean?" she asked.

"Well, it will be hard for me to remember how many days in a row you come in on time, so I put these up to remind me. I thought that might also help you to know how many days you have left for the challenge and me dancing on a table in each of the wings of the contact center."

Her eyes opened wide and she said, "You're kidding."

I just smiled and replied, "Tomorrow when you come in on time, just tear off the '30' and toss it on my desk, and then you'll see that you have 29 more days to go until I dance on the table… since you will be here every day on time."

She lifted the stack of papers that were on the nails and saw the "1" on the last page of the stack.

I said, "I have to go to a meeting. I will see you in the morning at 7am sharp."

The next morning, there was a knock on my office door. It was Tammy and she was smiling. I looked at my watch: 6:58am. I heard the rip of the piece of paper that had a "30" on it. She walked into my office and put it on my desk.

Since Tammy's emotional need was to get approval and attention from others, she was happy to tell people about the challenge. Hundreds of people in departments across the organization knew about the challenge. Everywhere Tammy went in the building, people were asking her about it. They even started to encourage her. I would walk down the hall and see people congratulate and "high-five" her. Each morning, she would rip off the top number and lay it on my desk.

People brought her coffee so she wouldn't have to stop on the way to the office. Somebody would bring her a bagel or a piece of coffee cake, so she wouldn't waste time eating breakfast at home. There were words of encouragement on Post-it notes on her computer. One team even hung up a piece of poster board that said, "We believe in you Tammy!" I watched in amazement as hundreds of employees got behind Tammy's challenge. People were coming by my office to tell me that they couldn't wait to see me dance.

Emotionally, Tammy needed to be acknowledged by people. From a leadership perspective, I knew that if she could meet the challenge, not only would she form a new habit, but the new habit could change her life. Further, what a great story she could tell others to inspire and help them through their challenges ("Third-Party Story"). Her success would encourage others to meet their goals.

Tammy loved the attention and got to day "20" of her challenge. I knew something was going amiss when at 6:55am I heard a commotion outside my office. People were running to find her. With one minute to spare, Tammy ran up to the shrinking stack of papers hanging outside my office and ripped the number "11" off of the nails. She peeked around the corner of my door and looked at me.

It looked like she had literally rolled out of bed, thrown on her clothes, and come to work. Her hair was usually in large ringlets, cascading down to her shoulders. Her makeup always looked perfect. Today, she had mascara under her eyes, her hair was a mess, and she looked totally disheveled.

I looked up at her standing in my doorway, smiled and said, "Congratulations, you are almost to your goal. I would hate for you to disappoint all those people out there rooting for you to be a success and meet this challenge. I know they are going to be disappointed if you don't make it. So, I'm glad you are here. Please remember that you need to be logged into your desk by 7am. Let me know how I can help."

She looked at me with tears in her eyes and said, "Thank you."

Tammy had a few close calls over the next 10 days. Once, her car wouldn't start and she called the receptionist, who quickly found someone who went and picked her up. Another time, there was an accident on the main road outside the office. Tammy parked her car on the shoulder of the road and ran the rest of the way to the office.

That final morning, a crowd of people came to the office to wait for her arrival. People even came on their day off. Others showed up outside their shift time. The parking lot was full, and people stood in two lines facing each other so they could cheer her on as she made her way into the building. Someone blocked off a parking space with orange cones, so she would have a place to park, just in case she was running late.

I stood by the window in my office and watched in amazement. Tammy arrived on time, and the parking lot erupted in applause. She walked through the two lines of people that extended almost halfway across the main parking lot. She was all smiles and was "high-fiving" people all the way to the door. When she got to the door, Tammy looked over to my office window and waved. Everyone turned to see what I would do. I put my arms up in the air like a football referee signifying a touchdown and the parking lot once again exploded in applause.

Tammy marched straight to my office. She ripped off that number one and walked over to the trash can near my desk. People lined the hallways, clapping. As she came over to me, we both began to cry. I was so proud of her. When it finally quieted down, she asked me, "You're still going to dance, right?"

"Of course!" I replied.

She looked at me and asked, "What if each shift doesn't have the opportunity to see you dance?"

"Well," I said, "then I had better dance multiple times today and multiple times tomorrow."

She smiled and gave me one more hug. She then turned around to the crowd, and announced, "Okay everyone, back to the work! We have customers waiting!"

I went back into my office and got the piece of paper that I had prepped for the occasion. It read, "She did it! – I always knew she could!" I signed my name at the bottom, went outside my office door and hung it on those two small nails.

They strapped the legs of four conference tables together for my stage. I had prepared a cabaret dance and danced multiple times that day and the next. Even though I really can't dance well, everyone had a great time.

Later that afternoon, Tammy and I had a discussion about why she felt she could complete this challenge when she previously couldn't. She said, "You figured out what made me tick the day when you asked me all the 'why' questions. That's when I figured out why I do what I do. The challenge was fun because it fed into where I was emotionally and," she added with a smile, "I wanted to see you dance." When she asked me how I figured out what to do to help her create a new habit, I told her about the "Meet Them Where They Are" tool in *The Leadership Toolbox*. She thought for a moment and said, "I use that tool but from a skill-set perspective."

I said, "I usually use it from a skill-set perspective too, but you were a special case." I explained that the "Dangle the Carrot" tool wasn't working with her. Even the possibility of a management position had not been enough to change the behavior. "I had to get creative with another tool."

Tammy had to make changes in her evening and morning routines to create new habits and accomplish her goal. She was an example to others and emotionally rewarded. A few months later, there was a management position opening. Once the announcement was posted on the bulletin boards, I noticed that people were writing her name on it. She applied, interviewed, and got the promotion. She truly had changed and made a lasting impression on the organization.

Take the challenge for your employees and "Meet Them Where They Are." When you do, you will be able to challenge them and get them to the next level. That next level doesn't necessarily mean a promotion. It could mean that they are happier in what they are currently doing. Either way, they are influencing others while growing in their skill set and professional maturity.

This tool can build self-esteem and confidence in your people and can create loyalty, so when situations get tough, people stay the course and become part of the solution. It will also deepen your leadership bench and get more people ready for promotions faster. It's a tool that requires you to think about each team member individually, since each person is in a different place. The "Meet Them Where They Are" tool can be combined with other tools in *The Leadership Toolbox* to establish a strong foundation and culture within a company. Utilize these tools together and you'll see great results in your people, your metrics, your customer base, and your bottom line.

Praise Calls, Emails, Texts
Build a Positive Chain Reaction
That Drives Rock Star Performance

One evening after work, I picked up my two small children from the day care center and headed home to make dinner. Tired from a long day, we carried the backpacks and my briefcase from the car into the house and I hurried to the kitchen. Thirty minutes later, as we sat down to the dinner table, the phone rang. I got out of my chair and answered the phone. It was my boss and mentor, Leon.

He said, "I know you are home with the kids and I don't want to keep you from them, but I just had to call and tell you what a great job you are doing. Your enthusiasm really pulls people together and I wanted you to know that I appreciate all your hard work." The call took me by surprise. It wasn't like he never thanked me at the office. We talked throughout the day, and each evening, he thanked me before I left. However, Leon was a creature of habit and this call was out of his routine, so I wasn't sure what he was going to say next. Still surprised, I managed to stammer, "Why... thank you so much."

He replied, "Well, I will let you get back to the family. Thanks again. I will see you in the morning."

My son must have seen my "tired and worn out from the day mommy face" suddenly change, because he said, "Wow, Mommy! That must have been good news!" I told them what happened, and he responded, "That must make you feel good, Mommy, because you are happy right now."

I instantly realized what an effect that telephone call had on me. Little did I know at the time that this first "Praise Call" would impact my career and become an important tool in *The Leadership Toolbox*.

That night, I thought through the emotions that I felt *prior, during, and after* Leon's phone call. It was only a 15-second phone call, but my entire attitude and outlook on the day changed within that very short period of time.

I wondered how I could create this type of feeling throughout my entire team, especially when they were experiencing a tough day. Would that change in attitude be enough to change their sales performance? What would the results be if all my leaders consistently utilized these types of calls, just as we had utilized "The Big Picture" tool? Could I duplicate and triplicate my efforts as a leader so that others could be inspired without my direct involvement?

"Praise Calls" is one of my favorite tools in *The Leadership Toolbox* for several reasons:

- It gives immediate gratification to the recipient and the initiator because they both see and feel the reaction that results from utilizing the tool.

- It encourages more of the same behavior from the employee, without directly asking for it.

- People that receive "Praise Calls" will talk about them, which inspires other employees to change their behaviors or enhance their performances in hopes of receiving their own "Praise Calls."

- When your employees are in different locations or your team works from home, the impact of your "Praise Calls" can go viral in chat or text within seconds, causing a chain reaction of positive attitudes and enthusiasm across your organization.

- It's foolproof and scalable inside any organization, no matter the size.

- There are many different strategies for utilizing this tool to get the maximum results.

Employee performance or behavior is the core of your "Praise Calls." Acknowledging top performers is the most obvious reason, but you may also want to recognize other things:

- Attitude or enthusiasm

- Teamwork

- Helping another employee

- A great idea

- Cleaning up in the kitchen

- Showing up to work on time two days in a row

- Making a presentation

- Getting the break room straightened out

- Improved performance

The list of possibilities goes on and on. Sometimes it is difficult to find something to praise an employee about, so get creative and be sincere. The result will be worth your efforts. Just the act of picking up the phone to tell them something positive makes a lasting impression. It provides encouragement that will continuously drive their current and future performance.

By utilizing the "Praise Call" tool, you can significantly increase the speed of the results you are trying to drive in your organization. The key to this success is the consistency with which you implement the tool. That doesn't mean you have to make a hundred calls a day to see profound results. You can designate 10 minutes a day to make calls or set a goal to make a certain number of calls weekly. Either of these options can still result in positive outcomes.

When I am driving something new in an organization or when we have a short time frame during which to move through an initiative, I will "front load" the number of "Praise Calls" I make. For example, I will do 10 calls the first day to get the enthusiasm spreading throughout the organization, and then will reduce the number of calls I make moving forward. Here are some quick case studies. Then, I will break down the methodology of the "Praise Call" tool so you can achieve the greatest impact without spending hours every day making calls.

Case Study I

I was hired to turn around the performance of a virtual/work from home contact center division. The wrong management team was in place. Negativity, chaos, and fear permeated the culture. Employee attrition and absenteeism were the highest I had ever seen within the contact center industry.

I got *The Leadership Toolbox* out and started to cultivate the culture I knew we needed to have to be successful. I utilized the "Praise Call" tool and personally called 100 customer-facing technical advisors per week for the first four weeks of my tenure. Within one month, I had placed 400 "Praise Calls." I know that may sound over the top, even for me, but the organization was about to lose their Fortune 500 client due to non-performance. A big impact was needed to stop the organization's normal behaviors dead in their tracks. I knew the sheer number of calls would go viral and drive a positive attitude across the entire organization.

As I made these "Praise Calls" during those first four weeks, I would watch the team chats light up with activity. Most people had never received a call thanking them or praising their efforts from someone at work, let alone a person in a senior leadership role.

I called Jennie, a woman who had just started with the organization. Her husband answered the phone. I told him who I was and asked to speak to Jennie. He yelled, "Honey, it's Vicki! I think you are getting a 'Praise Call!'" I couldn't help but chuckle.

When Jennie took the phone from her husband, she asked, "You picked me to call? Is this a 'Praise Call?'"

"Yes Jennie, it is a 'Praise Call!'" I replied.

"Oh my gosh!" Jennie responded excitedly. "I can't believe you are calling me."

I told her that her team leader said she was the most positive person on the team and an inspiration to her teammates. I told her that I appreciated her enthusiasm, thanked her again and we said goodbye.

Case Study II

While working in another organization, I called the monthly top-performing person on each team. On one occasion, I called Maryann. Her 10-year-old daughter answered the phone. I explained who I was and asked to speak to her mom. She told me that her mom wasn't available and then asked if she could take a message. I said, "Please tell your mom that Vicki called to tell her she rocks at work and that I'm so glad she is part of our team."

She told me that she would give her mom the "Praise Call" message. "You know about 'Praise Calls?'" I asked.

She replied in a matter-of-fact tone, "Everyone in our family knows about 'Praise Calls.'" Smiling, I thanked her and hung up.

The next day I got an email from Maryann thanking me for the call. At the bottom of the email were two photos. One was a drawing her daughter had made with the words: "Vicki says you ROCK and that she is glad you are part of the team." The other photo showed the front of the refrigerator where her daughter had posted the message. Apparently, after Maryann finished showering and dressing, her three children excitedly took her by the hands and led her to the refrigerator. They had rearranged all the papers on the refrigerator and had put the "Praise Call" drawing right in the middle. They proudly showed her the paper and then clapped for her. Maryann went on to say in her email that she was surprised by the profound impact the "Praise Call" had on her family. A month or so later, I received another email from Maryann telling me that her family was now regularly posting "Praise Notes" on the refrigerator to show their appreciation for one another.

As you are making your "Praise Calls," you may find that most people will not pick up the phone if they don't know who is calling. That's okay. Just leave a "Praise Voice Mail" with the same word choices. It can be just as effective as a "Praise Call." Trust me – they will program your number into their phones, so that they will know it's you the next time you call and will happily pick up. I chuckle when I call someone and picking up the phone they immediately ask, "Vic, is that you? I'm getting a 'Praise Call?'"

I gladly respond, "Yes, you are!"

You can use "Praise Calls" at every level on the corporate ladder. Try them with your peers when working on a project together. Try them with your boss. Give a "Praise Call" to someone in the benefits department to thank them for assisting you. The next time you have a challenge and need assistance, they will remember how well you treated them. By using this tool consistently, you will see the difference in the attitudes of your team and supporting departments. You will also see the positive effect in their performance.

Case Study III
Major Launches, Push Weeks and Struggles – Use a "Praise Call Campaign"

We were having one of the largest launches in the history of my tenure with a virtual/work from home business process outsourcing company (BPO). The client was a Fortune 200 international company that contracted us to answer technical support calls from customers. The hiring profile for these employees requested a high level of customer service, but strong technical support experience was not required. Because of this, it took longer to get the new technical support advisors trained since they weren't technically savvy.

For months, the organization had started hundreds of new technical support advisors every week or every other week, which posed a significant challenge. Because it took longer for these new advisors to absorb all of the training and be effective on the phone with customers, the customer service satisfaction scores across our entire organization dipped each time a newly hired group started taking customer calls. Additionally, veteran employees were being promoted from the front-line positions, which diluted the level of expertise and service being provided to customers calling in for assistance. Further complicating matters, about a hundred additional top-performing technical support advisors were removed from the phones to help the new advisors, which impacted customer service scores even more.

According to our contract with our Fortune 200 client, if our customer service satisfaction scores fell below a specific level, the client would subtract a specific percentage from our invoice. With a full court press and a massive number of new advisors on the phones, we had been maintaining our CSATs so far. We had started over 1,450 new customer-facing advisors, most with no technical expertise, in 90 days. However, when this last group of 300 new technical support advisors started taking customer calls, I was worried to the point where I couldn't sleep.

We had stretched the organization too much to keep our performance at the level we had promised this client. Normally, we were many percentage points above the minimum CSATs and were receiving performance bonuses month after month. But now, as the last 300 of the 1,450 new advisors started taking calls, I was concerned about our overall CSATs. I asked my business analyst to look at the historical and current data and to predict what our CSAT would be the last month of this current product launch. When he called me, he said, "Vic, it's not good." He explained that we would fall short of the minimum CSAT by three percentage points. I didn't say anything at first, but my brain was in over drive – failure was not an option.

I opened *The Leadership Toolbox* and called my senior team together on our conference bridge. My business analyst gave them the same information he had provided to me. I said, "I need your help and I need you to trust me. I want to do something we have never done before in this organization. I have to be honest. I have never done what I am about to ask at this level. I want to launch a 'Praise Call Campaign.' I want us to call all new employees in *one* day to get the momentum going and then do it again next week."

There was dead silence on the conference bridge. I added, "I know I am asking a lot. You are putting in tons of hours each week and now I am asking you for more. I will be in the trenches with you every step of the way. I need you to trust me on this. I know this will take us over the TOP ("The Big Picture")! Will you help me?"

One of my senior leaders said, "You know we are not going to tell you no. It's a lot, Vic, but if you feel that strongly, I'm in and I can speak for all of us. We're here. We'll do it."

Before I could say anything, one of my operations support team added, "We're talking over 300 calls in a day and there are only eight senior leaders doing the calling."

Someone else responded, "Well…that is a lot, so we better get off this call and get going."

Fortunately, when my team said they would do something, they did it. We all took our lists and started dialing. We made over 300 phone calls in one day, and the following week, we set aside a day to make another 300+ calls. At the end of the month, and by the skin of our teeth, we hit our CSAT goal. It was by .2 of a point, but we hit it!

I know without a shadow of a doubt, and my team would agree, that the "Praise Call Campaign" made all the difference in our performance. The calls got everyone excited and that excitement went viral, sweeping across our national virtual/work from home organization. Supervisors and other managers had "Praise Call Campaigns" going on with their teams as well. It was a huge push, and it worked. Harvard Business Review reports that happy people are 31%

more productive and have 37% higher sales. They are also three times more creative than their counterparts. How we feel at work has a lot to do with our results and the "Praise Call Campaign" proved it!

"Praise Call Campaigns" can work during the last days of the month when everyone is running for the finish line to get their key performance indicators accomplished. They can also be utilized after a big sales or push week, when people tend to relax once they have made their numbers. A "Praise Call Campaign" can spark re-engagement across the organization. Try calling your support teams at the end of the quarter to give them a boost of energy. An extremely effective "Praise Call Campaign" is calling everyone that showed up to work the day after a holiday, when a lot of people want a three-day weekend and call out sick. By looking for the gaps in your organization, you can likely identify several specific areas where the "Praise Calls" tool in *The Leadership Toolbox* can be helpful.

Nailing down Your "Praise Call" Methodology

When you first get on the phone with someone to do a "Praise Call," it's important to let people know immediately that it will be a short call. If you don't preface the "Praise Call" a certain way, employees will want to talk about whatever is on their minds. I love their enthusiasm, but the main objective of the "Praise Call" is to move quickly and give praise. By doing this properly you won't stop the flow of the call by saying, "I don't have time to listen to your ideas" or "That's not what this call is about. We can talk about that later." We want the conversation to stay very upbeat and motivational. Any type of comment that makes the employee feel negative or uncomfortable will negate the feeling you are trying to create with the call.

For the "Praise Call" tool in *The Leadership Toolbox*, I suggest the following intro. You can change the words to fit your personality.

"Hi _____, this is Vicki from the office. I'm just reaching out for a sec to tell you that I appreciate _____.
I value your passion and contribution. I just wanted to say thank you."

If you hear silence after you finish speaking, this means that the person doesn't know what to say. That's usually because they have never had a leader call and thank them before. When this happens, I generally wait a few seconds and say, "Well I appreciate you picking up the phone. Thanks again. Have a great rest of your day. Bye." If they thank me, I say, "You are most welcome. I appreciate you picking up the phone. Have a great rest of your day. Bye."

Remember, if no one answers, you can leave a "Praise Voice Mail" with a message that says exactly what you would have said if they picked up the call. People may change their cell phone numbers, so you want to be very careful when leaving a message. I never give the name of the company I am calling from. I also don't leave my last name or anything personal on a voice mail, even if I have spoken to them before. You can say, "It's Vicki from the office" or "It's Vicki from work." You can also just say, "It's Vicki." If a family member picks up the phone and the employee is not available, you can say, "Please tell him/her that Vicki from work called and I wanted to thank him/her for doing a great job. Thanks so much!" That's it. Don't provide any personal or detailed information.

Now, I realize that everyone isn't as charismatic as I am, but I have had people who are true introverts make "Praise Calls." The positive feedback is usually the fuel to keep introverted leaders dialing. I have made thousands and thousands of these calls in my career, and I have received positive reactions 100% of the time. "Praise Calls" are easy and quick to make and have a huge impact.

Case Study IV
"Praise Call Parties"

I took over a particularly challenging organization where the leaders in the company had been in their positions for years. The company had done well, but market conditions were changing and the skill set of the leadership team had not been cultivated. The egos of these leaders were connected to the accomplishments of yesterday and the CEO knew that this impacted his ability to drive the organization forward. These leaders were very passionate when telling me that they weren't going to try anything new.

I knew if I told them we were going to do "Praise Calls," they would roll their eyes. So, instead I invited them to a *party*. We met for lunch and had a great time. After we finished eating, I asked them if they would try something new. I explained that if they felt it wasn't worthwhile after trying it, I wouldn't ask them to do it again.

After I explained the concept of the "Praise Call" and broke down the methodology, we each made one call. I then went around the room to see what kind of response they had gotten from the person they had called. All of the responses were positive. I said, "Great! Let's do another one." We all dialed, and then I went around the room again and asked for feedback. I could hear the enthusiasm in their voices as they explained how the "Praise Call" was received on the other end of the phone.

I asked Sally, who had been the most negative person in the room when we first started, to take the lead on moving through the "Praise Call Party." She nodded and said, "Okay, let's make another call." After we all were done, I nodded for her to continue. Sally went around the room asking each leader for feedback. With only three rounds of calls, the attitudes in the room had changed. This was also motivated by the fact that Sally, who was always so negative, was smiling.

When we were done, I uncovered a special bakery box with a decadent, multi-layer chocolate cake in it. Everyone laughed, and I asked Sally to cut the cake. The tension was gone, and everyone had a great time. By the end of the "party," they were talking about the future and what we could accomplish.

We used this "party" system to drive so many projects in my tenure with that company. Just be creative and make it fun. When we duplicate our "Praise Call" efforts, we have more employees receiving "Praise Calls" and enthusiasm spreads. It's from these feelings that people come to work excited and anxious to get projects done on time. They feel happy to talk with customers, which leads to more success and fuels more excitement. "Praise Calls" can create a positive chain reaction in the organization, which affects key performance indicators, including revenue and net profit.

Departmental "Praise Call Campaigns"

In another company I was hired to turn around contact center operations where there was also tension in between departments. We used "Praise Call Campaigns" from my customer service teams to call people in other departments. The CEO told me that he saw a dramatic difference in the attitude between departments from the very first time we utilized this tool. We continued our Departmental "Praise Call Campaigns" once a quarter, calling team members in other departments to keep the doors of communication open. Interdepartmental support is crucial to a successful organization and departmental "Praise Call Campaigns" can be a real asset that reaps huge rewards.

Being Creative

The "Praise Call" tool in *The Leadership Toolbox* can be used in chat, email, and text. A word of caution though: If you are putting something in writing, make sure you change up your word choices. Out of excitement, recipients may forward or cut and paste the text they receive from you to others. If it is discovered that you are just telling everyone the same thing, the praise text, chat, or email will lose its impact and people won't trust you.

I know that we exist in a world where some people live on text messaging; however, a phone call catches people off guard and increases the element of surprise. If necessary, you can use multiple channels to communicate, but I recommend that you use "Praise Calls" as your first channel. It may sound old school and take a bit more time, but the impact is greater due to the recipient's emotional response to hearing your actual voice.

If I do choose to text, I generally do so in addition to my "Praise Calls." Make your texts straight to the point. For example:

- Great meeting. Loved how u presented!
- Wow! U amaze me w/your creativity!
- Another sale! U inspire so many of us!
- Know I called u earlier, but just wanted to say congrats again!
- Wow – Great presentation!

Make the words your own and remember that the important thing is to get praise moving within your organization. I challenge you to try one to three calls and/or texts a day for a month and watch how the enthusiasm spreads and results in performance change. It will take you less than 10 minutes and will be well worth the effort.

A Positive Chain Reaction – You Can *Feel* the Difference

Think about the impact you can make with one "Praise Call" and two "Praise Texts" per day for five days within your organization:

One "Praise Call" and two "Praise Texts" per day for five days (Total of 15 calls),

and if,

three additional leaders each make one "Praise Call" and two "Praise Texts"

per day, for five days (Total of 45 calls)

that would mean,

that 60 individuals in your organization would be receive a "Praise Call"

or a "Praise Text" within a five-day period,

and if,

each of those 60 people that received the praise told just one other person,

there could be 120 people in your organization

affected in a positive way.

These numbers are conservative. People usually tell more than one person when something wonderful happens to them, especially if it's unexpected. Think about the possibilities for a national or international organization where people are utilizing this tool. The "Praise Call" tool in *The Leadership Toolbox* pulls teams together, raising the positive energy and enthusiasm across your organization. People work faster when they are happy, so production schedules can have days shaved off their projected duration. Fewer mistakes are made, and deadlines are met when your people feel emotionally validated. Customer-facing employees' positive energy is transferred to the customer experience. The number of safety days in a row in the manufacturing plant or warehouse can be increased. People work together better and show up on time for work. When people are happy, employee attrition is reduced, and not only is there a cost savings, but also less stress on all departments.

When this tool becomes part of the fabric of your organization, you will not only see leaders making "Praise Calls" and "Praise Texts" but other employees will pick up this tool and use it with their co-workers as well. Your chats, phone calls, company social media, and texts will uplift your employee base. This chain reaction will create a noticeable difference in your top and bottom lines.

Now, for those of you who believe it's not your job to validate your employees — that's okay. But *what if* "Praise Calls" could inspire and motivate your team so that each salesperson makes one extra sale a year? *What if* your absenteeism could be affected or your employee attrition decreased? *What if* your team could get the project done ahead of schedule because they felt more validated, happier and inspired with a new level of team work? Wouldn't it be worth a shot to try it?

I wouldn't have personally made thousands and thousands of "Praise Calls" in my career or have all my organizations make thousands and thousands of these calls over time if the results weren't there. Take the "Praise Call" Challenge for one month and see what happens. I'm confident you will end up with some great "Third-Party Stories" of success to share.

The Gap Tool
Duplicate Your Efforts to Move Faster, Without Increasing Labor Costs

During an interview years ago, a CEO asked me if I managed by "numbers." I told him that I believed numbers were important, but that I did not sleep with financials under my pillow at night. "My philosophy as a leader is that I better know that something is going south before it shows up on my P&L," I explained. "I don't like surprises."

Front-line employees and first line leaders will see gaps long before the numbers show up on a report. *The Leadership Toolbox* has a formal tool that is instrumental for addressing the gaps in your organization, while simultaneously increasing the leadership mindset of your employee base and providing on-the-job training to your leadership teams.

Emotions Connected with Employees' Ideas and Processes

Throughout my years of turning around contact centers and other operations within companies, I have formulated some basic observations when it comes to the emotions surrounding any kind of challenge within an organization:

- When people come up with concepts, products, services, technology, or processes, their egos can become attached to them, and their ideas become an extension of who they are.

101

- When there is a business need to question, tweak, or even do away with their idea or process, their egos can feel psychologically attacked. They can have all kinds of self-doubt, which doesn't feel good, so they hold on tight to their process or idea, which can result in a tug of war within the organization.

- People believe that once an issue has been addressed, it's crossed off their list and they don't want to revisit it.

- In some organizations, when front-line employees see things that aren't working, they may not speak up because they feel the company culture does not promote an exchange of ideas. This can lead to an unmotivated employee base, which inadvertently leads to less productivity.

- Some leaders believe that their culture promotes the exchange of ideas. If that is something you believe, I would challenge you to do a gut check and ask your people what they think ("The People Know the Answer").

The statement "I made a mistake" can leave a person feeling bad about themselves because they have attached their ego to the mistake. So, in my opinion, mistakes have no place in business. By changing our vocabulary, we can start to disassociate the ego from performance at work, so it doesn't get in the way. Once that is accomplished, we can look at business from a different perspective and reduce the time it takes to identify challenges and address them, so that we can move faster towards the goal.

In my organizations, we use the word "gap" instead of the word "mistake." Gaps in our business processes aren't mistakes, so we don't have to feel bad about them. They just need to be plugged or fixed. No emotions. We move our egos out of the way, so that we can look unemotionally at the gaps in the business and plug them. The tools in *The Leadership Toolbox* evoke positive feelings in your employees and leadership. By understanding the feelings and using a practical approach towards business, you can build a chain reaction of success and have fun while doing it.

"The Gap Tool" in *The Leadership Toolbox* is a systematic approach that anyone in business can utilize. It provides a way to identify and plug gaps inside your organization that will not only empower your people and teach them a new skill set but it can also stop a metric from going in the wrong direction, before it shows up on a report.

In one organization, my client was a Fortune 100 company that utilized a computerized invoicing system. My business analyst would submit our monthly invoice to an internal department in our company, where it was uploaded into our client's system for payment. As our business division continued to grow, our multi-million-dollar monthly invoices surpassed the page limit for our client's automated invoicing system. According to our contract, there was a financial penalty assessed on our total invoice amount if our client didn't receive our invoice by a specific date.

When I was notified by our client that they hadn't received the invoice, I was surprised. My business analyst had a confirmation email from our internal department confirming they had receipt of the invoice. After several phone calls to our internal accounting department, we were told that our invoice hadn't been submitted to our client because it had surpassed the number of pages in the client's automated invoicing template. The woman in our internal department followed procedure and sent an email to her boss alerting him that there was an issue. Unfortunately, he was on vacation for two weeks and she did nothing to further address the issue during his absence. Apparently, there was no written policy in the manual regarding what to do if your boss is on vacation. When her boss returned after his vacation, he also wasn't sure what to do, so he sent an email to someone else. I eventually learned that our internal department needed $50 to purchase additional "pages" for our client's invoicing template, but no one knew who should pay the fee. I guess that wasn't in the process either, so no one did anything. Obviously, there was a breakdown in process and communication.

My business analyst offered the use of his credit card to purchase the additional pages for the computerized invoice template, but his offer was declined because our company procedure required the use of a director, VP, or SVP's company credit card. I was in international waters on a cruise ship, so my business analyst went to the VP of the division, who got out of his chair and walked over to the accounting department to give someone his company credit card for purchase of the additional template pages.

Sounds ridiculous, doesn't it? But this type of situation happens all the time in business organizations. Fortunately, we were able to resolve the gap before any penalties were assessed. The processes were not connected with a metric that any executive was reviewing, so the gap went undetected. So many of our cost saving measures stay below the radar because they don't have a line item on our P&L, but they can affect revenue, costs, and ultimately, profit. I've consulted in companies that wouldn't streamline interdepartmental processes because they assumed it would take 18 months and a full-time project manager to drive the project. There are processes in most companies that can be streamlined to reduce your number one expense – labor costs. Addressing these costs improves the bottom line.

Our front-line employees are often the first to identify gaps within the organization. However, if we continuously ignore their warnings and fail to close the gaps, they will stop telling us about them. Employees become disengaged and begin coming to work for the sole purpose of checking off the boxes and finishing their daily duties. Soon a displeasing key metric shows up on a report and leadership wonders why they didn't know what was going on.

Case Study

I was hired by a contact center company that was having trouble meeting the performance expectations of their Fortune 100 client. Most of the 700 front-line employees and leadership worked from home. No one was talking about the gaps in this national organization because leaders were busy and just trying to make it through their day. The front-line employees had tried to tell upper management what was wrong, but no one listened.

The first-level leadership position is probably the hardest job inside of a contact center, so I went to the level of leadership that I believed would have the most information I needed to assess some of the "whys" behind the performance. I called a first-level team management meeting and spoke with 25 team managers on a conference bridge. I explained that I was hired to help get them back on track so they could salvage their relationship with their client and earn more business. I opened *The Leadership Toolbox* and started to pull out some of my tools.

- We wanted to improve our performance so that we could earn more business with this Fortune 100 client. ("The Big Picture")

- As the organization grew, we would need more recruiters, trainers, people to help new customer service agents, team managers, middle management, and people to run training roundtables. ("Dangle the Carrot")

- We needed money to pay for these extra leadership positions, so I explained that we needed to increase our invoice dollars. ("Make Money")

- We weren't going to throw money at a problem. We needed to be creative and do more with what we already had. ("Save Money")

- I acknowledged that they had been in the company longer than I had been and that they knew what was going on better than I did. For us to turn around the business unit, we would need to harness all of their great ideas. If we didn't do that, I was afraid we wouldn't be successful. I was depending on them to figure things out and let me know what we needed to do. ("Everyone Has a Sign on Their Head That Says, 'Make Me Feel Important'" and "The People Know the Answer")

I asked for a volunteer to jump up on the virtual whiteboard and take notes. A woman named Lori volunteered. I asked the team to start telling me where the gaps were. "For example," I explained, "if people aren't showing up for work – that's a gap. If people aren't proficient at taking a customer call after weeks of training class – that's a gap." I told them nothing was off-limits. I asked them to preface what they said with, "The gap I see is _____."

That's all I needed to say. The gaps came fast and furious. Lori was trying to keep up with everyone as she madly typed onto our virtual white board. About an hour later, we had over 70 gaps listed on the board.

There are several reasons to utilize "The Gap Tool" in this manner.

1. Everyone gets all the items they would normally gripe and gossip about out of their system, so there is no reason to spend more time complaining when they leave the conference bridge.

2. Participants feel listened to, which validates them as human beings.

3. They see their gap on the board and now it's official that the leader knows about the gap. ("The Mirror")

4. There is accountability for the leader to acknowledge and help drive a systematic approach to plug the gap. ("The Mirror")

I told them the next step was to categorize these gaps under headings that made sense. Lori was sharing her computer screen with all of us as she made the list and I asked her to pull up an Excel spreadsheet. We then took each gap and identified a category it would fit in. We quickly went through all 70 gaps and put them into appropriate categories.

At this point, these first-level leaders felt like they were working to fix a problem. You could feel the energy on the conference bridge. In less than 30 minutes, we had a workable document. There was complete silence for a moment until I said, "Wow! Great work, everyone!" ("Everyone Has a Sign on Their Head That Says, 'Make Me Feel Important'")

I went on, "Now, I know that you have been waiting for an opportunity to address these issues in the business and I bet you know what we should do to plug these gaps." ("The People Know the Answer")

I asked Lori to email the list of gaps to everyone on the conference bridge. Then I asked each leader to take the next few days to rank the categories in order of importance so that we knew what we had to work on first, second, third, and so on. The next assignment was to take all the gaps under each category and rank them on priority of importance. I explained that there were no right or wrong answers. I just needed to see what they thought were the priorities. I explained that we would have another meeting the first part of the following week to go through the results.

Before we ended the call, I reminded them:

- Where we were going as a team. ("The Big Picture")

- I needed their help because I couldn't do it by myself and they had more experience in the company. ("Everyone Has a Sign on Their Head That Says, 'Make Me Feel Important'")

- I was counting on them for more information as we attacked the gap list, so that we could plug these the gaps quickly. ("The People Know the Answer")

- Once we plugged the gaps with their solutions ("The People Know the Answer"), we would be more efficient. With more efficiency, we would have more time to mentor and develop our customer service agents, which would help our customers and move our customer service satisfaction scores in the right direction. ("The Big Picture")

- When that happened, our client would be happy and give us more business, resulting in more revenue for the company. ("Make Money")

- With more revenue, we would be able to offer promotions. ("Dangle the Carrot")

I thanked everyone for their assistance and ended the conference call. Over the next couple of days, they prioritized the gap list, sending the information to Lori so she could combine it before we met the following week.

Through the years, I have found that everyone usually agrees with what the core gaps are within an organization. Once you have five to six core gaps identified, then you can put the others in the "parking garage" to address later. I have found that when you plug the first set of gaps, some of the other gaps disappear because they have been plugged in the process or they have become obsolete. At this point in the process, people feel like they are moving in the right direction and become energized.

Once we had the gaps prioritized, I asked for volunteers to lead project teams for plugging the gaps. I explained that the project leader would steer each project and that the leader did not have to do all the work or have all the ideas. I emphasized that leading a project team would help cultivate new skills that would be necessary to move up the ladder into a position with more responsibility and compensation. ("Dangle the Carrot")

Although I believe in formal education, I have found that on-the-job training can gain traction faster. However, most companies don't teach first and second-level leaders how to manage a project, let alone a project that has input from other departments. Without these skills, leaders will not be ready for the next step on the corporate ladder, and when they are promoted, they will actually dilute that level of leadership in their business units. This can turn into a vicious cycle and affect results within a company. "The Gap Tool" teaches project management skills and how to gain agreement. It also uses actual challenges to provide opportunities for real time communication strategies among new leaders and those wanting to move up the corporate ladder. As with any of the tools in *The Leadership Toolbox*, we are mentoring leaders, so their new skill sets will drive the organization towards a chain reaction of success.

There are three different levels of participation in utilizing "The Gap Tool" – project team member, project leader, and resource for the team when assistance is needed. I asked each of them to think about how they wanted to help and to let Lori know. We then set up a date and time for another short 15-minute meeting. When I looked at Lori's sign-up list the next day, there were several situations where two people wanted to head up the same project. I talked with both people to see if they were willing to work together as co-leaders. If there were four people instead of three on a project team, that was fine. If there were six instead of four, that was fine too. There is no wrong number on a project team as long as it makes sense. When the members are passionate about a gap, they will have a lot of input and will feel responsible for the outcome.

In some instances, there were four or five gaps that no one volunteered to work on, which was also not a problem. The next morning, I explained the situation and told them that we could address it in one of two ways. Someone could move to lead that gap project team or we could move the gap to the "parking garage" for a later date. Remember, passion for closing the gap is critical. If people are passionate, they are invested in the outcome. When you have 70 gaps, like in this organization, you can't plug them all at the same time, so my school of thought is to follow the people's passion. They understand where the real rocks are in the road are, so trust your people. ("The People Know the Answer")

Working with project leads at all levels is a priority for me. It keeps me closer to where the action is, and I glean a great deal of information about the organization and the people. It also takes the open-door policy to a whole new level. People have told me through the years that they like seeing me all over the company because it makes them feel that I know what is going on and that I look human and approachable. Once everyone understands "The Gap Tool" they need very little interaction, if any, from me. Executives ask me all the time how I can move organizations forward as quickly as I can. It's because of *The Leadership Toolbox*. "The Gap Tool," as with all of the tools, creates a proactive chain reaction all over the enterprise and we move much faster that way.

Being a project leader usually takes one to two hours of work a week. The project looks great on a resume for a promotion ("Dangle the Carrot") and it gives participants a great story for their "Third-Party Story" library. Remember, passion is the key. When employees want to help plug a gap, they become excited and invested in the results.

In the end, we plugged the gaps, increasing performance and CSATs. We moved towards being a top-performing organization in our client's enterprise and earned praise from our client. The projects accomplished a few things:

1. Gaps were plugged that were causing inefficiency, pain, and unnecessary labor costs in the organization.

2. People were no longer complaining or gossiping about issues, so they weren't wasting time and taking emotional energy from their jobs.

3. They positively affected productivity, which had an impact on the customer experience, which in turn had a positive effect on our revenue.

4. They built confidence in the individual skill sets of the people and engaged employees so they wanted to come to work and help make the organization more successful.

5. They instilled a new mindset within the first-level leadership team that they had the power to identify and plug gaps in a systematic process-driven approach. This helped them look at their jobs in an entirely different way.

6. It created excitement in the team and got everyone on board for moving toward "The Big Picture." This built momentum, and we started identifying and attacking gaps, streamlining processes that affected our key performance indicators.

7. Project leads and team managers shared the gap projects with customer-facing employees, so that they could learn new skills as well. It also kept these front-line employees feeling like they were in the loop, so they were more engaged. This also reduced the amount of time wasted complaining and gossiping, so front-line employees were also more productive.

8. These projects built the organization's confidence in my leadership. It showed them that I cared and understood where they were coming from. It also served as my acknowledgement that there were things we needed to do to make the organization better and articulated my commitment to provide career growth for them. When they understood all this, the lines of communication opened, and no one hid anything from me. We had full disclosure.

9. We reiterated that gaps were not mistakes. They were business challenges, with no one's ego attached to them. We saved time in moving through issues and didn't have any emotional tug of wars in meetings.

When "The Gap Tool" becomes part of the fabric of your organization, it helps close gaps before they affect one of the metrics on your reporting. In my organizations, we even have front-line employees utilize the "The Gap Tool" and create their project plans with members of their own team, working on the gap projects in between customer calls.

I very seldom have any surprises on any metrics because front-line employees and leaders alert me to the fact that we have a gap. Then we can quickly plug that gap, so that it doesn't show up on a report, while also improving leadership skill sets throughout the organization. I can't be everywhere at once, so if everyone is on "gap alert," we can move more quickly.

Daily "Gap Analysis" for Maximum Results

You can use "The Gap Tool" every month or quarter to identify ongoing gaps in your business. But to get maximum results and literally change the way employees at all levels think and move through their workdays, my organizations use "The Gap Tool" daily. Again, we are creating a new mindset and habit that engages employees and promotes healthy participation in a company to reach company goals ("The Big Picture"). Identifying gaps becomes a badge of honor.

After the initial drive that generally occurs when I first arrive at a new company, I find that we no longer have big gaps because we identify them more quickly, so they are smaller gaps that don't cause much damage.

If there is a technology gap, you can get IT involved right away. Sometimes it is just a matter of a patch or a temporary workaround and the gap is plugged. If the gap involves the features of a piece of a software or hardware, the enhancement can be put on a larger IT project timeline or can be put on a technology list as part of future business requirements. In a nutshell, if everyone looks for gaps, you can streamline your operations and get ahead of real issues that can cause revenue, expense, customer service, or employee challenges.

How to Drive "The Gap Tool" and Make It a Mindset Within Your Organization

A strong communication strategy, especially the utilization of videos, can be a catalyst for driving strategies within virtual/work from home and multi-site location environments. You can never utilize *The Leadership Toolbox* enough. The more you talk about the tools, the more ingrained they become inside the organization. These strategic videos help keep the entire company engaged and feeling like they are part of the solution. It also portrays transparency in my leadership style, which employees say is part of why they trust and follow me.

The *Individual* "Gap Tool"

One of the benefits of "The Gap Tool" is that it can affect the attitudes of the employees in the organization and the way they think about what they personally do at work each day. The word gap takes the ego out of the equation. Since gaps are part of every business, employees can identify the gap in their own personal performance, come up with a game plan, and plug the gap.

When I utilize "The Gap Tool" inside my company or when hired as a consultant, I have seen increases in the use of the word "gap" throughout the organization. The most profound place to find this is at the front-line employee level. I have had salespeople say, "Vic, I have a sales gap. Can I get some additional help?" Employees that are on a final written warning have said, "I have a gap in my productivity and need someone to help me."

Because the ego is not involved, the gap in their personal performance can easily be talked about, with no shame or embarrassment. That means that no one feels the need to hide their "mistakes." We talk about gaps like we talk about the weather. It is a liberating experience that engages your employee base, enhances your organization's teamwork, and helps move performance metrics in a positive direction.

Does "The Gap Tool" Take a Lot More Time out of Your Day?

When I'm asked this question, I usually respond, "You are going to spend the time in one of two ways. You can spend the time being proactive by fully utilizing "The Gap Tool" and taking the time to move through gaps, OR you can spend the time on the back end when things go side-ways and you are having to initiate damage control. Either way, you are going to spend the time."

When organizations stumble, it costs money, time, and wear and tear on the people. So, why not be proactive? When we harness the energy of employees at all levels, we not only teach them new skills, but we reinforce the organization's culture, which builds momentum. Leaders at all levels and even "front-line employee pseudo-leaders" can benefit from utilizing "The Gap Tool." This tool in *The Leadership Toolbox* is a way to become more efficient and nimble, so that you can react to changes in market conditions, and increase employee engagement, revenue and bottom line contribution.

Pilot Programs
Harness New Ideas and Build Your Leadership Bench

A CEO hired me to turn around performance in his company's contact center operation. As with most of my consulting and formal positions throughout the years, this organization was about to lose its largest client, a consumer goods company. The current sales conversion for our client's flagship product was 3%. Bill, the president of the consumer goods company, would call every morning and demand a new game plan to move his sales conversion to at least 25%. We had hundreds of minimum wage salespeople answering calls from his potential customers, but they weren't meeting his sales conversion expectations. Since I was brand new to the company, I didn't know the first thing about his products, but I did know I had to do something quickly to salvage this account.

I opened *The Leadership Toolbox* and took out "The People Know the Answer" tool and "The Gap Tool." I then talked with salespeople from the contact center operations floor. I noticed a consistent pattern in the information they reported, which allowed me to reach some conclusions relatively quickly. First, the salespeople were instructed to read a script that didn't make much sense to them. Second, the infomercials didn't give the price of the product, so potential customers experienced sticker shock when they were informed about the cost. Third, it was obvious that potential customers didn't trust the company. I listened to many of the live calls the salespeople were taking and was horrified by what I heard.

I called Bill and gave him all the information the salespeople had given me. He wasn't surprised. Responding in his usual demanding and argumentative manner, he said the salespeople told him the same thing during his last visit to our contact center. He insisted that they were "just salespeople" and that he was the subject matter expert on his products. I strongly suggested that we move to a bulleted talk track instead of a scripted conversation, letting the salespeople come up with word choices to personalize customer interaction and increase sales. I opened *The Leadership Toolbox* and asked him if we could do a few "Pilot Programs" to try some new talk tracks with small groups of salespeople and see if we could increase sales conversion. Reluctantly, he agreed.

I went back to my teams and gave them the news. Three front-line sales people stepped up to run three separate "Pilot Programs" comprised of eight salespeople each. The project teams put different talk tracks together, which the management team and I approved. Over the next week, we saw the sales conversion increase from 3% to 7%. The teams continued tweaking their talk tracks and, by the end of the fourth week, we had come up with three final versions. The "Pilot Program" teams suggested that we give each salesperson the ability to choose which talk track they preferred using. I thought that was a great idea because it put the power back into the salesperson's hands, allowing them to take charge of their own destiny and performance. We rolled out all three talk tracks over the next few months, and sales conversion rates went from 7% to 33%. The client was ecstatic!

The success of the "Pilot Program" affected more than just sales though. The self-confidence of the front-line agents grew because they felt that the client had listened to them. They also told me that their confidence in the client's products and our own company increased as well. They appreciated having more control over their own performance and the amount of commissions they could earn. We saw paychecks increase, with some salespeople doubling their minimum-wage compensation through commissions. You can imagine the electrifying atmosphere in the organization when that happened.

"The Gap Tool" Drives the "Pilot Program" Tool

When "The Gap Tool" is utilized to identify gaps within your organization, your team will want to try different ideas to see what will successfully plug them. Some ideas are simple; others are more complicated. Everyone has an idea, so my attitude is this:

"If it's legal, moral, and ethical and it doesn't cost the company an employee, a client, a customer, or a boat load of money, let's try it!"

A "Pilot Program" is a concept or process that is going to be tested in a small group within your organization to see if it works. Open *The Leadership Toolbox* and utilize "The People Know the Answer" and "The Gap Tool" as a foundation to the "Pilot Program" tool. This causes a chain reaction of success within the organization – all driven by the customer-facing employees. When "Pilot Programs" become part of your organization, employees at all levels start actively looking for gaps. They utilize "The Gap Tool," then implement "Pilot Programs" to plug them.

If a "Pilot Program" doesn't provide the result we are looking for, or it can't help the organization move forward, we just toss it out. There are no egos attached to a "Pilot Program." Even more importantly, it doesn't take the usual company committee to approve a new initiative. "Pilot Programs" are very small. They are a way to see if an idea is worth pursuing. They are not intimidating and don't take a lot of money, if any. All the data is collected, and the teams tweak their "Pilot Programs" until they either 1) decide they work or 2) decide they don't work and stop doing them. Once they have a "Pilot Program" that works, they can roll it out to a few more teams (tweaking it if necessary), and then roll it out to a few more teams, until it becomes a part of the current approved process within your organization.

Throughout the years, I have seen challenges and gaps come up in an organization and watched leaders develop massive projects to fix them. The process of fixing the gap can get in the way of plugging the gap because it takes forever to get new projects approved. First, a project manager is hired or assigned. Next, groups of people are assembled in many departments, which may create scheduling issues. These projects usually have a sizable price tag on them, so money needs to be found and budgets prepared. They can also be extremely time-consuming, dragging on for weeks or months. Meanwhile, there is a major gap in the organization that may be bleeding revenue, resources, productivity, and customer satisfaction. These gaps and challenges also drain the energy of your teams, causing members to feel distracted and frustrated. In other instances, I have seen it take months to get a project up and running. By the time the project is halfway through, people realize it won't fix the issue or the market has changed, and the project no longer makes sense. Again, wasted resources and time.

"Pilot Programs" in *The Leadership Toolbox* can be set up quickly. The small pilot team can work through the hiccups that will come up unexpectedly.

It's a learning process which pulls the team together and gets them thinking differently about business. It also creates an effective training and mentoring environment for your organization. I have found that "Pilot Program" leaders gain valuable skills and that these "pseudo-leadership positions" are a great stepping stone to becoming effective first-level supervisors.

Acknowledging Discomfort When Trying Something New

At first, there may be an internal tug of war with yourself as you allow front-line employees to try new things. You may even decide to utilize the "Pilot Program" but then have trouble letting go of the reins. You may worry that the lack of skill set among these employees will make a mess that you will eventually have to clean up.

However, if the "Pilot Program" process is followed, and you as the leader are kept abreast of the progress, you will become more comfortable with utilizing the tool. Your teams will create new skill sets that will be practiced and perfected, their professional maturity will increase, and your confidence in their abilities will grow. When that happens, you are duplicating your efforts over and over, creating a chain reaction of leadership development within the organization. Results can then be showcased in videos, displayed on bulletin boards, or on your company intranet to create excitement and spur more employee engagement within the organization. These accomplishments will also help you become more comfortable with "Pilot Programs" and more willing to trust your front-line employees with them.

Ingredients of a Successful "Pilot Program"

The goal is to have your front-line employees in every department identify gaps in real time and come up with a "Pilot Program" to plug those gaps. Some "Pilot Programs" need assistance from supporting departments, including IT, human resources, and sales. Remember you will get better results, gain more momentum, and increase skill sets if you utilize front-line employees in these departments as well.

It's best to ask for volunteers when starting "Pilot Programs," which is a great way to identify leadership qualities in your employees. This also helps with the productivity of these employees. I almost always require high performance as a prerequisite for participating on a "Pilot Program" team. In my experience, volunteers will move through their regular job duties faster and better in order to work on one of these coveted programs.

Measurable results are essential for "Pilot Programs." When I arrive at an organization and start discussing "Pilot Programs," I make certain to review and approve each program before it begins. I sit down with the volunteers to instill the reason for the "Pilot Program" and the goal we want to ultimately accomplish. Without this information, employees may not be able to evaluate whether or not the program is successful. I usually request a measurable result. The timeframe is also discussed and agreed upon, although it can be reduced or increased based on results. It's a mentoring process that gets their leadership mindset growing.

Here's a list of some questions that can help you and your team as you decide which "Pilot Programs" to initiate:

- What is the reason for the pilot?
- What do we want to see accomplished from the pilot?
- How will we know if and when the pilot is successful?
- How will we measure progress and success?
- How long will the pilot last?

Other questions I like to ask are:

- Which other departments will need to be involved?
- How much cost, if any, will be involved?

To develop a stronger leadership mindset among my employees, I may also ask about how the pilot will affect:

- Our customers or clients
- Our team
- Our brand in the marketplace
- Our company culture
- Our gross revenue
- Our bottom line

In some organizations, I have passed out this list so employees could ask themselves these questions before presenting a "Pilot Program" idea to management.

Your "Pilot Program" may sound great, but I have seen situations where someone from the IT Department asks the right questions, and the "Pilot Program" is dismantled because it was not feasible. In some cases, a front-line technology person might invite their director or vice president to one of the "Pilot Program" meetings for ten minutes. Since directors and VPs usually have more knowledge and insight into the company's strategic plans, they can quickly add information that is critical or move an obstacle out of the way. It's amazing what can happen when they come into a "Pilot Program" meeting for a few minutes.

When other departments work with your department on a "Pilot Program," make sure to acknowledge them with "Praise Calls." You will find that the people in these other departments will feel validated and become motivated to help you with ongoing initiatives.

"Pilot Programs" are easy to launch because they are less threatening to everyone's time and company resources. They are psychologically easier to handle and less daunting. We're just trying something to see if it will work. We tweak and tweak, handling challenges until the process is perfected. Sometimes "Pilot Programs" are only in place for a limited amount of time to get through a difficult period in an organization's growth process. I routinely use "Pilot Programs" for product and holiday launches, when we want to try new ways of getting front-line employees trained and working faster.

Some "Pilot Programs" may be intended to last for longer periods of time, but team members decide to stop them midstream because they don't make sense. It becomes apparent that the project is too labor intensive, or it doesn't give them the desired result. Because "mistakes" are now gaps, there is no ego involved and no one feels bad. The "Pilot Program" has no personal feelings of its own, so people learn and move on. It's a very refreshing process and one that receives easy buy-in from employees.

Case Study

Doing large ramps and seasonal surges inside a contact center environment can cause real challenges in maintaining customer service satisfaction (CSAT) performance. In one of my larger organizations, we created a "Pilot Program" that could take below-average performers and cultivate them into superstars – in a short period of time.

Paul, my Quality Assurance Manager, loved the idea of utilizing the "Pilot Program" tool in *The Leadership Toolbox*. Due to an upcoming product launch, and the number of new customer service representatives (CSRs) in our organization, the customer service satisfaction scores were struggling. Paul picked 12 CSRs with below-average CSATs (between 70%-75%) for participation in a "Pilot Program." Within six weeks, every one of these CSRs went from 70%-75% to over 90% in CSATs.

I asked him to do another "Pilot Program" with the same project team and help 20 different CSRs, instead of 12 – with no additional leadership, trainers, or coaches. Six weeks later, all 20 CSRs went from 70%-75% to over 90% CSATs.

Paul was rather impressed with the program results. I praised his performance but also told him that, since we were growing so fast, we needed to step it up a bit. I asked him to take another 20 people from 70% to over 90% CSATs in *five* weeks. When he commented that it was impossible, I said jokingly, "Really? You're going to tell me you and your team can't figure out how to tweak this so that you can do it in five weeks instead of six? I'll let you tell your team they can't figure it out."

Paul laughed and replied, "Well, you do have a way with words – we'll figure it out."

Five weeks later, another group of 20 CSRs who were struggling with their CSATs went from 70% to over 90%.

I called Paul and complimented him. "I am going to ask you to take another 20 people from 70% and move them to 90% in *four* weeks."

He didn't hesitate. "I knew you were going to ask me that. Already been thinking about it."

Four weeks later, 20 CSRs went from 70% to over 90% CSATs.

Paul then called me and said, "I think we should do *two* teams of 20 customer service representatives and get them from 70% to over 90% in four weeks."

Four weeks later, both teams hit 90% or above in CSATs. Then they took on the challenge of training three teams, and they succeeded as well. In the end, we had figured out how to take 60-100 people at a time and move their CSATs from below-average to over 90% – which was above-average performance!

I showcased these "Pilot Programs" in my videos to my national virtual/work at home team, so front-line employees could follow the process and the results of each "Pilot Program." This caused a surge of excitement. Customer-facing CSRs were begging to be put on these "Pilot Program" teams. We even had a waiting list! We were complimented by our Fortune 100 client and received performance bonuses on our monthly invoices – month after month after month. The client even asked us to share our process, since our performance was so impressive. There was a sense of pride in working on a "Pilot Program." Participants even created "Pilot Program" team names and these teams began competing with each other.

In using my weekly videos to showcase the "Pilot Program," I highlighted:

- Future growth and additional promotions would come as we grew and earned more business from our client. ("The Big Picture")

- Since most people want to go to work for a company that offers growth opportunities, we would be able to make promotions, which would afford them more opportunities! ("Dangle the Carrot")

- The Quality Team and the CSRs who participated in the "Pilot Programs" all worked on the process and ultimately contributed to the success. ("The People Know the Answer")

- We never would have been as successful without this "Pilot Program", which allows everyone to share in the credit. ("Everyone Has a Sign on Their Head That Says, 'Make Me Feel Important'")

- Since we were a top-performing organization working with an international client, we were earning monthly bonuses on our invoice and had the capital to expand. ("Make Money")

- We utilized our leadership development candidates to help with the programs and used informal leaders. ("Save Money")

- Each CSR, leadership development candidate, and Quality Team member had a "Third-Party Story" for their resume or to use in interviews, as they applied for other positions within the organization. ("Third-Party Story")

We utilized "Praise Calls" within these "Pilot Program" teams, creating even more excitement. CSRs wanted to be part of these "Pilot Programs" as they swept through the organization. Everyone in the organization wanted to see how long our streak of 90% CSATs in these "Pilot Programs" would last, and they wanted to be part of the success.

Once the "Pilot Program" tool in *The Leadership Toolbox* gets embedded in the minds of the people in your organization, you will have front-line employees trying "Pilot Programs" in their immediate teams – and who knows – they may come up with an idea that results in huge rewards for the company.

"Pilot Programs" – An Addition to Your Leadership Development Programs

Like all of the tools in *The Leadership Toolbox*, the "Pilot Program" tool can become a part of leadership development within your organization. "Pilot Program" leaders can present what they have accomplished to their supervisor or a small group of supervisors. When they do this, they are utilizing the "Third-Party Story" tool to articulate the business situation that was a challenge to the organization, the action they took ("Pilot Program"), and the results. This is real on-the-job training. They can also showcase what didn't work in the "Pilot Program" and why it didn't work. This builds more professional maturity and leadership mindsets within front-line employees. As these employees learn new skills and get promoted, they will be adequately prepared for that next move, and their peers will be more likely to support their promotion. Even employees who are not on the actual project teams will learn from observing. Utilizing *The Leadership Toolbox*, your organization can experience a chain reaction of success that moves your company forward much more quickly than the executive team ever thought possible.

"Pilot Programs" can be a vital part of moving an organization through rough waters or improving a process that is just no longer working. This tool builds excitement that drives teams towards "The Big Picture." There is minimal cost (if any) associated with utilizing this tool and it can reap big rewards for every level of your company. Skill sets of the front-line employees are increased and a new level of professional maturity is cultivated. Not only can you increase productivity and revenue with the "Pilot Program" tool, but your customers will benefit from better service, and improved product and service offerings.

Recognize the Behavior
You Are Trying to Drive
Identify Metrics Going the Wrong Way
Before They Show up on Your Report

In one of my senior-level management positions, I had the interesting opportunity to lead both operations and business development. I asked the business development representatives to document their weekly activities in the customer relationship management system by Sunday evening of each week, so I could analyze our sales pipeline and prepare my weekly executive summary.

All of the business development representatives made sure their activities were well documented in the system, except for Keith. I constantly had to chase him down for his numbers, which were usually written on a notepad or on Post-it notes stuck to the dashboard in his truck. Once I tracked him down, I practically had to stand over him while he put his numbers into the system. As a result, it often took me an additional two hours every Monday to get my executive summary ready. I was frustrated. To make matters even worse, Keith was my top-performing rep. I always gave him slack, because he could "sell ice to an Eskimo." Keith was great at cold calling on prospects and could get into any door, in any business. He built great relationships with prospects and clients, and his sales numbers were fantastic. Everyone loved Keith, including me, but I had to find a way to get him to document his numbers in the system on time.

I talked with Keith multiple times. He admitted that putting his activity into the system was a problem for him and that he was unorganized. I had one of the other reps work with him in the field to demonstrate how he could put his activity into the system throughout the day in real time. Still, there was no change in Keith's behavior.

I opened *The Leadership Toolbox* and grabbed the "Everyone Has a Sign on Their Head That Says, 'Make Me Feel Important'" tool. I tried phrases like, "everyone looks up to you" and "I really need your help" but, the following Monday, there was still no documentation in the system. I thought about threatening to fire him but feared that the threat wouldn't work – and I would have to fire him to keep my creditability. I even told him that he was causing me stress, which almost made him cry because he said I was the best boss he'd ever had.

Keith was an open book and told everyone he was struggling. Utilizing the "Recognize the Behavior You Are Trying to Drive" tool, I started posting "My Congratulations Notes" on the bulletin boards in each of my locations to recognize the reps who completed their reports on time. To be honest, I thought this was a bit over the top because I'd never tried this with a business development level employee. I didn't even think it would work, but three weeks later, Keith finally had his numbers in the system. I did a "Praise Dance" (no, that's not a real tool in *The Leadership Toolbox*) while I was alone in my office and I made a "Praise Call" to Keith.

I never said a word to the team or to Keith about the recognition. I just did it. As Keith's participation increased, the team automatically cheered him on. Keith eventually created a new habit, and I had less stress because I was able to get my executive summary ready on time.

Behavior Drives the Action or the Metric

The metrics that show up on reports are directly related to employee behavior. The behavior is the "signal" that will guide you along the way. If you can understand and recognize those "signals," then you may be able to prevent a key performance indicator from going in the wrong direction or encourage behavior that drives a metric in the right direction. If we aren't being proactive, we may be too late in our efforts to stop a metric from sliding in the wrong direction. By reinforcing positive employee behaviors, we can keep metrics strong or even move them into stronger positions.

Let's say your employee absenteeism is too high, or maybe it's just average, and you want to reduce it, then absenteeism is the metric you are trying to change. The behavior of an employee determines the absenteeism rate. Therefore, by influencing the behavior in a positive way, you can move that metric in the right direction.

You could utilize the "Recognize the Behavior You Are Trying to Drive" tool to reduce absenteeism by recognizing the people who show up on your team every day. For example, you could place a thank you note on the employee's desk, workstation, or office. In larger organizations, you could place people's names on a physical bulletin board with a personalized note. In virtual/work at home environments, you could use your organization's communication board to "Recognize the Behavior You Are Trying to Drive." You could also send an email to a specific team or department with everyone's names on it who showed up for work the day before, with a big "Congratulations" written across the top of the document. As with "Praise Calls," utilizing multiple channels to publish the recognition enhances the "Recognizing the Behavior You Are Trying to Drive" tool.

Now, you may be thinking this will take a long time to do every day, but you can delegate this task. It doesn't have to be done company wide. Try a "Pilot Program" with a couple of department heads and see how things go. Remember, you are going to spend the time either way. You can be proactive up front and "Recognize the Behavior You Are Trying to Drive" or you can wait until you have a real crisis on your hands and then send your team to do damage control.

You don't need to have a big contest. No big announcement. No fanfare. Just start posting the names of the people who exhibit the behavior you are trying to drive with a big "Thank You!" You can even "sign" the document instead of printing your name. No explanation. Nothing else. It's human nature that people want to be validated ("Everyone Has a Sign on Their Head That Says, 'Make Me Feel Important'"), so the "Recognize the Behavior You Are Trying to Drive" tool can have a big impact.

Let's go back to the absenteeism example. As more and more people get their names on the "Thank You" board, it will inspire others. Meanwhile, your employee absenteeism metric is moving in the right direction. Some employees may tell you that it doesn't matter if their names are on the board, but trust me, people want positive recognition. If tardiness is an issue in your organization, then use the "Recognize the Behavior You Are Trying to Drive" tool for employees who show up on time. This doesn't have to be an ongoing process. Just utilize the tool when needed, for as long as it makes sense.

Case Study I

I took an assignment inside a business unit that was barely meeting their minimum performance metric and was far from being recognized as a top-performing organization. The goal was to get to top-performing status as quickly as possible. I set up four different strategy sessions – one for each level of leadership. I asked each of these teams which metrics they wanted to work on. Once we had a list, we prioritized it and reduced each of the three metrics down to specific behaviors that were negatively affecting the metrics. The first one was attendance.

Marilyn, one of the supervisors, decided to utilize the "Recognize the Behavior You Are Trying to Drive" tool to reduce her team's absenteeism. Each of her team members would come by her desk to say hello before their shift started. Once they got to their desks she would text them and say, "Thanks for coming in today." She would also add another behavior that she wanted to encourage, such as having a positive attitude, helping a new salesperson with one of the steps in the sales process, or encouraging a team member who was struggling with sales.

The team started to reinforce the same behavior, without even being asked, by launching a new salesperson 100% attendance initiative. Her team's attendance became one of the top in the organization and, to Marilyn's surprise, this accomplishment only took a few weeks to achieve. We also saw a 27% reduction in enterprise-wide absenteeism.

Case Study II

I was hired by a CEO to build a contact center solution for a business unit. Since a lot of the reporting was still being done manually, I spent time with the technology team, working to get the reports automated. The numbers for the reports came from multiple systems and it took the team hours to do the weekly reporting. The IT team was in the process of building out the technology system, so that they could integrate the data from various systems into one. For the moment, I received paper reports on my desk in the late morning, which made it impossible to provide reporting to my East Coast clients early enough in their day.

The IT team did an amazing job with what they had, but people were just plain tired and worn out. It was taking longer and longer for them to get the reporting accomplished each day and I kept asking for more data for my growing organization. They told me they felt like they were swimming upstream without a paddle and I could definitely sympathize with them.

Since I knew that the IT team was exhausted from my constant requests for more data, I decided to use the "Praise Call" tool. It helped a bit, but I needed something else to achieve the desired impact. I opened *The Leadership Toolbox* and decided to piggyback the "Recognize the Behavior You Are Trying to Drive" tool on top of the "Praise Call" tool.

One morning, I noticed that the report landed on my desk at 10:31am. I took an 8-1/2 x 11-inch piece of paper and wrote in big, red letters "10:31am – Thanks Everyone! You Rock!" I signed my name at the bottom of the sheet and posted it inside the IT bullpen.

When Derrick from the IT department delivered the reports the next morning, he asked me why I put up the time and thank you note in the IT bullpen. I told him I appreciated that the reports were delivered by 10:31am. That's all I said.

The next day they shaved seven minutes off the time. So, this time, I made two 8-1/2 x 11-inch notes, one for outside my office door and the other one for inside the IT bullpen. I put "10:24am. Wow! I'm impressed! Thanks so much!" and I signed my name at the bottom.

Over the next few weeks they started shaving time off the report's arrival time each day. Soon the report delivery person was literally running to give me the reports. As he ran down the middle of the large open room environment, the people in supporting departments would cheer him on.

Less than a month after I started posting, the manual process was more than an hour faster *and* the VP of Technology told me that the automation process was moving along faster than he thought was even possible. In fact, the project was moving so quickly, he had someone go in and check to make sure things were going in the right direction without any mistakes.

Once we had the reports automated, the IT team insisted on running my reports every morning and having them on my desk by the time I got to the office at 6am. As a reward, I threw them an ice cream party.

I had given no directive to get the reports completed earlier. The employees were not slacking in any way. All I did was "recognize the behavior I was trying to drive." They knew I respected their process ("The People Know the Answer") and of course, I praised them with "Praise Calls." Everyone felt good about the situation ("Everyone Has a Sign on Their Head That Says, 'Make Me Feel Important'") and the results were there.

It's Easy and Effective

There are so many behaviors that you can recognize in your organizations. Whether you are in the finance department, administration, technology, manufacturing, marketing, human resources, logistics, operations, sales or any other part of your company, you can identify which behaviors influence a metric or specific situation. Once you do that you can start "recognizing the behavior that you are trying to drive." Don't let the simplicity or the fact that people will "know what you are doing" deter you from giving this tool a try. Yes, this is an easy tool, but it is also very effective.

The tools in *The Leadership Toolbox* have been created to use as building blocks for each other, building a chain reaction of activity that will inspire success within your departments. Once you are consistently using the tools, they become part of your organization's fabric, influencing activities and behaviors that drive more effortless, positive change. It's because of the tools in *The Leadership Toolbox* that I feel teams can tackle anything and successfully make it across the finish line.

Try Before You Buy
Build a Leadership Bench
That Guarantees Future Success

I was hired by a CEO to come into an organization that was struggling to meet performance expectations and was losing money in their U.S. operations. They had been hired by a Fortune 500 company to answer customer technical support questions. Within my first week of attending meetings at all levels within the organization, it became apparent that the director, managers, and assistant manager teams spent the first half of each week figuring out why performance had been subpar the previous week. By Wednesday afternoon, the director and her management team provided their answers to the VP of Operations, who would then direct her internal teams on how to conduct damage control. On Monday of the following week, the vicious cycle would start again. The VP was driving damage control and managing in arrears, gaining no traction on turning things around. It was easy to see right away that this was a weekly exercise, so that the VP could prepare answers for her Fortune 500 clients, who were also asking the same questions. This had been going on for months and was a vicious cycle, that provided no increase in performance.

While I realize that understanding where you have been and how you got there are important questions to ask, the real issues were that 1) the organization suffered from the outdated management model that has managers telling people what to do, with absolutely no buy-in from customer-facing employees or first-level leaders, 2) the director and management teams didn't know how to duplicate their efforts so they could efficiently gather the information they needed to give to the VP, while simultaneously driving new strategies for the new week, and 3) some members of the management team were not a right fit for their current positions.

The director and management teams were frustrated and voiced their concern to me. The merry-go-round of requests and activity was causing a huge amount of stress, and they were gaining no traction in turning things around. During my one-on-one discussions with members of the management team and the director, they mentioned that there were better ways to handle this. When I asked each one if they had talked with the VP about a better method, they each replied, "She won't listen."

Through my years, I have seen many people frustrated with their management or their boss for doing things a certain way while at the same time believing they could do their boss's job if given the opportunity. In fact, most people feel they could do their boss's job *better* than their boss. So if people are thinking this way, we should use this thought process to our advantage. If the people in our organizations feel that they can do our jobs, then why don't we let them help? As a leader, what if there were two of you…three of you…ten of you? What if you could duplicate your efforts without increasing labor costs? This is one way you can get a chain reaction of success multiplying throughout your organization to increase performance.

Case Study I

I was working as a general manager in a business-to-business environment and was fortunate to have a great account manager in my organization. Cathy was a champion at cultivating strong business relationships with our clients. When she managed an account, revenue grew. She was one of those employees you wish you had ten of.

One of our accounts was IBM. The IBM teams loved Cathy and I was thrilled to see the account revenue ticking upward as it became one of our largest revenue generators. One afternoon, Cathy walked into my office and told me that she had been offered a job working for a software company. It gave her a great opportunity to make more money and work from home, which was extremely attractive to her as the mother of a one-year-old daughter. I couldn't even come close to the compensation they offered her, and even though her current position could have been done from home, I knew this was a golden opportunity for Cathy. She was touched and grateful that I was on board, but I said to her, "I am worried about the IBM account, so I am sure you have a transition plan."

She smiled and replied, "I already have a four-week plan to wean myself out of my position."

My mind was already whirling. Who would take her place? I didn't have anyone in the office who could be trained and working at full capacity in four weeks. I know that when clients have a great relationship with an account manager, it can be difficult for them to get used to a new person. There was revenue risk associated with Cathy's departure.

Cathy must have been reading my mind because my thought process was interrupted when she chuckled and asked, "Do you really think I would trust the IBM account to just anyone? I have already been training my replacement."

A look of shock covered my face. Cathy laughed and told me that Kari was ready to take on the account. "Kari? You have got to be kidding," I said. "She hardly says a word in meetings. She's got great skills…but Kari? Are you sure? No! Absolutely not!" I said, answering my own question.

Cathy softly said, "We have worked together for a while, Vicki. Please trust me. I totally believe in Kari. I've been taking her out to IBM for months. You said we needed to be ready for tremendous growth and duplicate ourselves, so I have been getting ready. I didn't know this opportunity with the software company would open up, but thankfully, I have been training Kari ("The People Know the Answer")."

I looked at her and said, "Cathy, this isn't about filling out paperwork. This is about driving overall strategy and thinking about what the client needs *before* they know they need it. Kari isn't on the same level as you."

Cathy replied, "Please trust me and talk with her." I looked at Cathy and said, "Okay, I will talk with her."

The next day, Kari came into my office. Before I could say anything, she said to me, "I know I am not your top pick. You've never seen me talk much. I'm sort of a wallflower, but I want this job. I have been working with Cathy for months on this account, getting ready for growth. I have been going to the client site for the last couple of months. I even have a whole new wardrobe to look the part. You said that desire is really important. I want this job so bad I can taste it. I want a chance."

An hour later, Kari left my office. I had agreed to give her 30 days to demonstrate what she could do. Cathy and Kari went back to IBM the next day and the handoff began. Two and a half weeks later, Cathy walked into my office and said the weaning process was complete. We threw Cathy a going-away party, and Kari took over.

During the next six months, Kari launched the strategy she and Cathy had been working on. The account grew at a faster pace than I expected, and I saw Kari's skill set grow before my eyes too. As she came out of her shell, I saw her warm personality and great sense of humor emerge. I went out with her one day to visit IBM, and I watched in amazement. Kari was a totally different person than I had seen six months earlier. The IBM teams loved Kari.

As all of this was unfolding, I discovered that Cathy had been an inspiration for other account managers in my offices and that each office was utilizing this approach. They were not only training their replacements and getting ready for growth but their protégés were increasing their skills in their current positions as well. No wonder revenue had doubled in less than a year. We were duplicating each manager's skill set. Even front-line employees were given an opportunity to learn parts of account manager duties, which increased their skill set, their leadership mindset, and the professional maturity in their current positions.

This is a very basic example of the "Try Before You Buy" tool in *The Leadership Toolbox*. It should not be confused with cross training, where you train an employee to perform another employee's duties in case of absenteeism from work. The "Try Before You Buy" tool is meant to help people increase their leadership mindset and professional maturity. It is for those people that aspire to be promoted within the organization. When utilized across your company, it will cause a chain reaction of success that will do more than just increase your leadership bench. As I have demonstrated throughout this book, my teams have consistently been able to accomplish the "near impossible" and this tool is one of the reasons why.

The Secret to the "Try Before You Buy" Tool

The foundation of this tool takes me back to earlier in my career when Leon, my mentor, told me that if I didn't have someone watching me do every aspect of my job, I would be missing a valuable opportunity to train and mentor. For over 20 years, I have given employees at every level of my organizations opportunities to perform duties from the jobs they wanted, even while doing their current jobs and before being formally promoted. My organizations have done this without adding to their headcount or working outside of normal manager-to-employee ratios. When you utilize this tool, the workload of your current leadership will decrease. They will find that they have more time, and they can now mentor more leaders – without increasing labor costs.

The "Try Before You Buy Tool" works for a number of reasons:

1. The candidate can try a portion of their manager's position in small steps, taking on more and more responsibility, which builds their confidence.

2. The candidate gains understanding of what their direct manager does in their day-to-day activities and they gain exposure to challenges in real time. You can see how they react to stress and challenging situations when they don't have all the information as well as how they treat people.

3. The team gets to see multiple team members, and in some cases, everyone on the team do a piece of the direct manager's position. With the right culture, which can be cultivated with *The Leadership Toolbox*, this promotes teamwork, without creating a competitive environment.

4. It becomes obvious who should have the next promotion because others on the team will start going to that candidate for assistance.

5. The candidates must be top performers and in good standing with the company, and this encourages people to perform so they can participate. Your metrics and key performance indicators will increase automatically while you utilize this tool.

6. There is a new strategic awareness to the entire team because people have a piece of the manager's job.

7. Because people want to be in this program, these leadership candidates work faster and harder on their regular jobs so they can do the extra tasks, increasing productivity naturally.

8. The manager has more time to mentor and develop new leadership but also to learn some of their manager's job.

9. There is no cost to your budget. No one is given a formal promotion at this point, and there are no increases in compensation. These duties are temporary. In fact, you might even move some of these duties around each month to see team members' different strengths and to find out what each person loves to do.

10. The entire team is energized, and it gives everyone a change of pace so their day-to-day work does not get monotonous.

11. Human resource professionals love this tool because it cultivates more employee engagement and organically creates authentic inclusion.

You may be thinking that you don't have time to put all of this on a schedule. In my contact center organizations, the scheduling and tracking of these activities is done by one of the candidates in between taking customers calls on the phone.

Over the last 20 years, I have utilized many variations of the "Try Before You Buy" tool. Here's what I have found:

Fewer than 50 percent of people that we "Try Before We Buy"

are promoted. The reason? Most can't do the job.

They can do their current jobs wonderfully and can still be successful with some additional duties but can't do the job in its entirety because it's just not a match for them. Some of the "Try Before You Buy" candidates decide they don't want to do the job and voluntarily give up their extra duties. However, in trying these new duties, a new mindset and level of respect for their manager, and for leadership in general, has been developed. Perhaps there are other duties they can temporarily try in another department or for another position.

The beauty of this program is that you don't have to formalize it. You utilize the "Pilot Program" tool in *The Leadership Toolbox* and start by asking a few of your managers to list the three job duties that are the easiest to teach for training purposes. I recognize that there are certain human resource management tasks that can't be handed off to a leadership candidate, but be creative. I always say it's not *if* but *how* you can successfully utilize this tool. Since this is a "Pilot Program," you don't need an in-depth plan. Since it's not a formal position, you don't need a formal job description or a compensation analysis.

As with all the tools in *The Leadership Toolbox*, there is a chain reaction of success as more and more people want to get involved. All must be top performers to participate so that your organization's performance increases. I have been told that people are afraid they are going to miss something exciting if they don't come to work when this tool is used regularly, so absenteeism within the organization goes down.

There are so many variables with the "Try Before You Buy" tool. Here's a real out-of-the-box case study that turned out leaders within one of my larger organizations as we were expanding rapidly.

Case Study II

I met Jack and personally mentored him when I was developing a new business solution for a contact center industry leader. Jack was smart and savvy, and had a very analytical mind. After I left the company, Jack made the decision to go back to college full time and quit his job. About a year later, he was working part-time and called to ask if he could come work with me.

After catching up for a few minutes, Jack said to me, "What if you hired me as a part-time manager? I could run one of the teams in your virtual contact center in just 20 hours a week. That means you would pay me half of what you pay your current front-line leaders and still get a top-performing team. In fact, give me your worst performing team, and it will be number one in your organization the first full month I am there." He didn't give me time to say anything and went on, "I know your standards are high, Vic, and I know you probably haven't done this before, but I am ready to give my two-weeks' notice at my current job today and start in two weeks. Come on, Vic. I can do this, and you know it."

I opened my mouth to speak, but he continued before I could say a word. "I will 'Try Before You Buy' and get someone ready to take on another team, so you're getting a great manager and a mentor for your organization at half price because I am only working 20 hours a week." Jack laughed. "I know you well enough to know that you will try this and take the gamble and bet on me. What do you have to lose? If I can't do it in the first 30 days, I will resign. You know I will find several leadership candidates in that 30 days, so you win either way and I get my chance…so when do you want me to start?"

Jack was right. The idea did intrigue me. I was in a huge turnaround situation in a virtual/work at home contact center environment and was getting ready for a product launch at the same time. Jack had no virtual/work from home experience, but he was right; I would rather gamble on him. If anyone could do this – and I was doubtful anyone could – he could. So, I agreed to his "Try Before You Buy" proposal.

Jack gave his notice and came in two weeks later. He took some front-line training and began taking customer calls. Two weeks later, I gave him the bottom-performing team out of the 19 teams from one of my business units. This team had 20 technical support advisors. Jack started handing off parts of the leadership duties for people to handle in between customer phone calls. This way, he had more time to mentor and coach more people. Customer-facing advisors on his team volunteered to move their schedules around because they wanted an opportunity to help with some leadership duties and an opportunity to be coached by him.

The first full month he was there, his team, even with brand new customer-facing advisors and low performers, went from 70% in customer service satisfaction scores (CSATs) to 90%, becoming the number one team in the organization. Everyone got excited.

Jack came back with another idea. He asked me to give him another 10 new and low-performing front-line technical support advisors, bringing his team to 30 members. His plan was to take Randy, his top leadership candidate, off the phones for 20 hours a week, so he could spend time mentoring him. That way Randy would assist with leadership duties and be learning some new skills while still being compensated at the advisor rate of pay. He finished off his sales pitch with, "So you are only paying me half of what you pay your other leaders because I am only working 20 hours a week instead of 40, *and* the advisor-to-manager ratio of 20-to-1 is still intact because Randy is taking on leadership responsibilities that equate to half of a manager." He went on, "I will be giving Randy an opportunity to assist me, and we are 'Trying Before We Buy.' Randy knows that he may not make the cut and be a manager during the next ramp, but he will be helping non-human-resources-related functions, so there is no risk. Plus, I will be teaching him about the other tools in the toolbox, so what do you have to lose?"

I hesitated. Jack sounded logical, but could he do it? After thinking it over for a minute, I replied, "Heck…why not?"

So Jack got Randy, his leadership development candidate, off the phones for half of his shift to help with the now 30 technical support advisors. Randy thought someone else should help as well, and he gave 10 of his mentoring hours to Mary so they could have double the brain power. This meant that both Randy and Mary each had 10 hours of leadership development time and 30 hours of taking customer calls, still keeping the manager-to-advisor ratio intact. When the next month's rankings came out, Jack's team was over 90% CSATs and was number one in the entire organization. My phone rang again.

"Hey Vic, it's Jack. I am so proud of the team. Aren't they doing a great job?"

I said, "Yes, you and the team are doing great!" I could tell by the tone of his voice that I had better brace myself.

Jack went on, "Why don't we push the envelope a bit? How about giving us another 10 people and another 20 hours of off-phone time for two 'Try Before You Buy' candidates? That gives us four leadership development candidates, each off the phone for 10 hours a week and on the phone the other 30 hours in the week. The manager-to-advisor ratios are still intact, and you are still just paying me for 20 hours a week. I have plenty of help. Why don't we give it a try?"

I said, "Sure why not?"

I placed a few calls to some of the members of Jack's team. They were excited. Some were hoping that they could become the next candidate and show Jack what they could do to help others. I knew most people couldn't do what Jack was doing. It took a certain kind of mentor and someone who was very organized. I asked Jack what he thought about the process so far.

"I am organized," he said, "but I don't do the candidate duty and coaching schedule. In fact, one of my technical support advisors does both schedules in between calls so that I don't have to waste 'off-the-phone mentoring time' for the leadership development candidates. She's really organized. I don't know what I would do without her. And Vic, the best part is that she loves doing it. It demonstrates how we work with each person's strengths. It gives her an opportunity to shine and it really helps the team out."

The following month, Jack's team was number one again. He asked me for 10 more people, and I went for it. By this time, one of the candidates had decided that management wasn't for them and went back to their normal duties. They went back to the phones full time and did "Praise Chats" to the team in between calls. I appreciated Jack's creativity in using multiple tools to drive performance.

The following month, his team was number one again. He was getting newly hired technical support advisors every month, and his team was still hitting its performance out of the ballpark. After four months, he was at 60 people. He told me that he wanted to come to work full time, while going to college. Of course, he gave me a great sales pitch and I brought him on full time. He grew that team to over 80 customer-facing advisors and continued to be number one month after month. His ratios of 20 customer-facing advisors to 40 hours of leadership time stayed intact, but we had no additional management compensation because 1) this was a temporary assignment, 2) people didn't have full management responsibility, and 3) the leadership development candidates were only off the phones for 10 hours a week when trying new responsibilities.

Performance was great because to be a "Try Before You Buy" candidate you had to be a top performer with your customer service satisfaction score and have great attendance. That helped drive revenue up and absenteeism down. When people felt they couldn't do a leadership duty or they didn't like it, they went back to answering phones full time. However, they did so with a new appreciation for their supervisors, an increased leadership mindset, and a greater level of professional maturity. They continued to help the team and drive performance.

Through this "Pilot Program," Jack developed leaders and generated a lot of buzz within the company. People from all over the organization begged to get onto his teams, and he could quickly find new leaders with a lot of potential, although only about 50% of these candidates were successful and promoted into formal management positions. Those successful candidates were thrilled to receive a promotion with full management compensation and their own team.

They had proven to management, themselves, and their team members that they had what it took to get results. Even those who were not promoted appreciated the opportunity to help, even though it didn't work out.

For the company, we were able to avoid the loss of financial resources and performance that results when the wrong employees are promoted to management. Ineffective leadership takes its toll on a team. Just because someone can do their current job well doesn't mean they are cut out to do the next level job. This "Pilot Program" can change the mindset in the organization. People become more engaged, have fun, and work well together, as they try new leadership duties. Key performance indicators are influenced in a very positive way because in a "Try Before You Buy" environment, people are energized.

Score Big Wins for You and Your Company

I have never found a downside to this tool. We provide the leadership training modules that "Minimize Risks," like sexual harassment and proper coaching documentation in the system. This additional mindset brings heightened awareness that benefits the organization. Supervisor positions are not for everyone, but candidates that don't make it in a formal management setting still take all the knowledge they gained back to their current positions, so that they can continue as a top-performing customer-facing employee. Their new appreciation for the leadership mindset benefits the employee as well. Utilizing the "Try Before You Buy" tool may even reveal that these employees are better suited for other areas of your company. Trying out different duties allows them to figure out what they love to do and to become more engaged at work.

No matter where you currently stand on the corporate ladder, ask yourself this question: "If *I* wanted a promotion, would I be willing to help my manager if it meant expanding my skill set and perhaps getting a future promotion?" The "Try Before You Buy" tool can put your leadership development program on the fast track. Try it as a "Pilot Program," and see what happens. Ask your leaders where they feel they need assistance and what duties can be handled by someone else ("The People Know the Answer").

The "Try Before You Buy" tool can be used in combination with many other tools in *The Leadership Toolbox*. Be creative. It "Dangles the Carrot" because employees can only participate if they are top performers. This is one of the reasons why Jack was able to hit number one CSAT status month after month after month. "Try Before You Buy" participants feel validated because "Everyone Has a Sign on Their Head That Says, 'Make Me Feel Important.'" It can get you ready to handle a holiday or product launch, which can drive your "Big Picture," and what great "Third-Party Stories" your candidates will have for their next interview!

Employee engagement is an extremely important initiative within the human resources department. I have found that human resource professionals will set the stage for the "Pilot Program" tool and the "Try Before You Buy" tool, paving the way for your organization to be successful. As these programs evolve, they can become valuable components of your company's leadership development.

As with all of the tools in *The Leadership Toolbox*, this tool builds a chain reaction of success and helps identify the right people to promote without wasting time and resources. Runaway emotions and disappointments are reduced as we set people up for achievements that reap huge rewards for employee engagement and satisfaction, the customer experience, revenue, and bottom-line contribution.

Triage
Gain Efficiencies While Simultaneously Increasing Employee Engagement

I was hired by a large international company to help mentor leaders and turn around struggling performance in their multi-site contact center organization. This organization was also expecting a 50% increase in customer calls and chat volume for the holiday season. We utilized "The Gap Tool" and identified a gap that would require enhancement of a software application that was necessary for efficient scaling of the organization. I made a few phone calls to the IT department to find out how difficult our request would be and got the thumbs up that it was an easy fix. I contacted the Director of Operations and explained that the IT department could make some minor changes in the software application but that they had a few questions. I suggested a short "Triage" and explained that this was a short meeting with a different kind of agenda and pace. It was for times when we needed information quickly. I estimated a "Triage" duration of 15-20 minutes for this issue.

The Director of Operations emphatically told me that there was no way he was going to have another meeting. I told him that I understood and suggested that the front-line supervisors answer the IT department's questions. He told me he wanted to be in all meetings but couldn't handle anything else on his plate, so the issue would have to wait until the weekly staff meeting scheduled for the following week. Since his organization was my client, I pulled back to see how they would handle the process.

During the next weekly interdepartmental staff meeting, I explained the situation. When I finished speaking, there was a collective relief that the fix could be so simple.

After the meeting, I asked Ellen, a first-level operations supervisor, to address some of the IT department's questions. She answered their questions via email and the IT department responded with another question. When Ellen received the email, she didn't understand the question, so she sent another email back asking for clarification. The IT department returned with clarification and a few other questions. She then answered the original question. However, the additional questions were something she had no idea about, so she emailed the contact center manager, only to receive the out of the office autoresponder.

I could go into the painstaking details about the email craziness that continued for over *three weeks*! You can imagine the "reply to all" emails going back and forth around the organization, filling up everyone's inboxes. Every week I gave an update in the weekly staff meeting, as the Director of Operations had requested. The VP finally gave a "Let's get everyone pulling in the same direction" motivational talk, yet the email craziness continued. I had an extremely difficult time with all of this. We were wasting payroll dollars and time, and details were falling through the cracks. I must admit, at this point, my lack of patience was getting the best of me.

I informed the Director about some of the challenges and why I was going to hold a "Triage" meeting. I called the head of the IT department and asked that he send a representative to a "Triage" meeting the following morning. I invited three other people from a couple of other departments, including operations, to attend. In one 15-minute "Triage," we exchanged all the necessary information and scheduled the final user test.

For the next *two weeks*, the emails flew back and forth about the user testing. Mind you, the user testing consisted of one person in a department putting information into the system and two other people from different departments trying to log in and view the inputted data. Simple, right? Apparently not. I finally stepped in and pulled everyone into another "Triage." In just 15 minutes, the test was completed. The technology enhancement was approved by the IT department and we were operational. It was utilized by multiple levels within the organization and saved hundreds of manual work hours.

At the next weekly staff meeting, I reported that the enhancement was working, and everyone cheered. It was like climbing Mount Everest, and I'm not a climber. The amount of time spent sending emails was staggering, yet the entire issue was resolved in two "Triages," totaling about 30 minutes. We wasted so much time, not to mention the stress on the people with the email craziness and the manual process that had leaders at three levels of the organization working longer hours.

Most people would agree that communication is key to moving an organization forward or trying to drive a project. However, people tend to prefer the path of least resistance. We work in a business climate where texts, emails, or updates to the project plan often replace real-time, verbal communications. Then people seem surprised when there is a misunderstanding in the message or update. Progress is stalled, employees and leadership become stressed, and we waste valuable time trying to move forward, in some cases adding labor hours to a process that is already costing the company money.

I have found that the "Triage" tool makes a huge difference in efficiency and ultimate success. In fact, once an organization is exposed to this tool in *The Leadership Toolbox*, they use it consistently to keep everyone on the same page. In today's electronic age, with software applications that keep us connected and virtually in one place, there is still nothing like talking to each other. If there is a gap while on the "Triage" call, it can be discussed immediately and a decision made quickly, saving everyone time.

People usually shudder when I first bring up this tool because they think it will take more time away from their already busy day. But as with many of the tools in *The Leadership Toolbox*, I look at it this way – you are spending the time either way. You can send emails and texts back and forth, creating frustration and delaying success, which usually means it's costing you money and more time, or you can be proactive and have a "Triage," which cuts down on stress, engages employees, and proactively moves things forward faster.

"Triages" are quick, fast-paced meetings and, like most of the tools in *The Leadership Toolbox*, can be utilized by all levels of leadership, including front-line employees in departments who have first-hand knowledge of the gaps in the organization and how they can be plugged.

When I went to work for another Fortune 500 company, the organization was not meeting contractual obligations to their clients. I asked the department heads from each department that touched my organization to send a front-line supervisor to a "Triage" meeting each morning. In 30 seconds to one minute, each department presented the highlights of any challenges or help they needed. I can't tell you how many gaps were plugged immediately during these "Triages." Everyone felt a sense of accomplishment and pride that numerous crises had been avoided because we connected first thing in the morning.

"Triages" are also a great training ground for supervisor or front-line employees to learn how to be concise and to the point when speaking. It is also a fantastic way to emotionally connect departments. This can be especially important in virtual/work at home environments or when there are multiple locations involved. The "Triage" tool in *The Leadership Toolbox* pulls people together, helps with leadership development, and helps plug gaps that hinder success.

Quick Case Study #1

I was hired to turn around an organization where one of the challenges for the outside sales organization was that they weren't meeting their sales conversion target. One of the first suggestions I made was that we meet as a team for a quick "Triage" each morning and get the game plan going. This added 15 minutes to their day, but by the moaning and groaning on the conference bridge you would have thought I told them they had to work every weekend.

We set up a calendar and I asked each sales person to lead the "Triage" on a specific day. As Leon, my mentor years ago used to say, "Either you need the meeting, or the meeting needs you." I told my team that they didn't have to be in the office or at their desk for the "Triage." In fact, I didn't care where they were – driving their children to school, getting ready for work, eating breakfast in their car, or working out in the gym. The "Triages" worked because they were short in duration, pulled people together as a team, and gave them the freedom to be wherever they happened to be at the time of the meeting. People chuckled when they heard kids in the background of the call or someone huffing and puffing while doing leg presses at the gym. It gave the "Triage" a different feeling and people were grateful they could continue their normal morning activities while still participating. The atmosphere was relaxed, and the team was more focused during the day, resulting in increased sales conversion. A few months later I tried to cancel the "Triages," but the team saw the value and didn't want to let them go.

Quick Case Study #2

In one of the larger virtual/work at home contact center operations I led, we were doing an operating system upgrade. Each of our over 1,500 technicians had to download the application, which took more than an hour, and install it manually to their computers. This had to be completed at the right time by each technician so as not to interfere with incoming customer calls and our agreed upon schedule with our client. In most multi-billion-dollar companies, a professional project manager from the Project Management Office (PMO) would be assigned to manage this type of project, but I decided that we would manage it ourselves.

If the upgrade didn't go off without a hitch, the technician would not be able to answer customer phones calls. Every minute they couldn't take a call, we would be losing revenue. In this organization, all of the front-line customer-facing technicians worked different shifts on different days, with their schedules changing weekly. Some employees worked part-time, and some worked a full-time schedule.

My organization was extremely nimble and had learned how to move quickly when utilizing the tools in *The Leadership Toolbox*. The IT department raised their eyebrows when I told them we would handle the project management ourselves. They asked, "Are you sure, Vic?" I told them I was sure. It was easier to do it ourselves than to try to bring a formal project manager up to speed about our operations and processes. We were moving fast, and our processes were rock solid. I knew we could handle any crisis that came our way.

Communication is critical in any organization, but it's very different driving change within a virtual/work at home environment or when you are leading multiple locations. From experience, we knew that we could never communicate too much. Our virtual bulletin board was updated in real time so that everyone could go to one central place for updates. We utilized "Team Triages," "Leadership Triages," "Shift Triages," and "Departmental Triages." Individual team bulletin boards for our almost 200 teams were also utilized. We had checks and balances at every step of the process, with back-up processes so that nothing could fall through the cracks. We even had "Communication Triages" so that each piece of the rollout strategy was communicated efficiently using videos, chats, texts, phone, and dialer messages.

In the end, the head of the IT department told me that even his team couldn't have driven communications the way we did and that in his 20 years in IT, he had never seen such a smooth rollout. As you can imagine, with over 1,500 people working in 40-plus states, all with different shifts and from their homes, there were challenges. However, the "Triages" were scheduled in advance with the appropriate people from every part of the entire organization, so we were able to quickly handle anything that came up unexpectedly and then make the appropriate decisions.

The operating system upgrade was a huge success. Challenges were addressed in real time with "Triages," the communication strategy went off without a hitch, and employees were engaged. There was a sense of personal and organizational pride that we could accomplish anything. Our employees weren't distracted and didn't take their eyes off the customer experience, which reflected in our CSATs. We stayed a top-performing organization, winning kudos from our Fortune 500 client.

My client asked me how we accomplished the systems upgrade so successfully, on time and faster than any other vendor in their international organization. As always, it was the same simple answer – "It's the people and the tools. They make all the difference."

Quick Case Study #3

I was hired as a contractor to turn around a brick and mortar contact center that was opened for the holiday season. The leader had been fired and I had just a month to get things turned around before Christmas. There was no communication strategy, and the team of about 350 front-line agents knew things were not going well. They were afraid they were going to lose their jobs.

I started doing "Employee Triages" at the beginning of every shift, starting at 6am. Shifts started every half an hour from 6am to 1pm and from 3pm to 5pm, seven days a week. Since time was of the essence, I came up with a communication/motivation "Triage" format. The front-line agents were asked to log into their computers, come to the front of the contact center for a quick 5-minute "Triage," and then start taking customer calls. I had a small white board at the front of the "Triage Center" and anyone could post information or a question. We addressed these at each "Triage."

Some of my more charismatic employees came up with a "Big Picture" cheer that agents utilized at the end of every "Triage." I taught the supervisors how to conduct these short meetings and then we asked top-performing agents to hold some of them. We moved the organization to top CSAT performance within a few weeks. Communication and motivation were key to this quick turnaround.

The client was surprised at the quick results and assigned three managers from their corporate headquarters to figure out how we accomplished the "fastest turnaround" they had ever seen. They looked at customer call patterns, our schedules, and the skill sets of our customer-facing advisors. After looking at everything they could think of, the vendor manager came into my office shaking his head and saying that they just couldn't figure it out. I pointed to my white board, where the five tools that we had utilized from *The Leadership Toolbox* were listed. He looked at the board, looked at me and shook his head, saying, "That's impossible. No way!" before walking out of my office.

Quick Case Study #4

I was hired as a consultant to help streamline an internal help desk for a 650-seat virtual/work from home contact center. The help desk schedules were not efficient, causing long wait times for customer-facing agents who were calling in for assistance. The current help desk reporting was not helpful in analyzing the performance and call patterns, and the customer-facing agents were frustrated with the lack of knowledge the help desk employees demonstrated.

I called a meeting and requested that there be a representative from every department on the conference bridge. Utilizing "The Gap Tool," we came up with a couple of "Pilot Programs," and started our action item list. I chose Larry, one of the assistant managers who showed a lot of promise and was looking for another promotion, to tackle this project with me.

I explained to everyone that we would have a "Triage" every day for the first week as we moved through the project plan. I gave them a couple of "Third-Party Stories" that showcased the "Triage" tool, and they enthusiastically said they would give it a try. As I mentored Larry, we met prior to the "Triage" to discuss how he would approach it and debriefed when it was over. After the first week, he asked this project team if they felt one more week of daily "Triages" was appropriate before weaning back to three "Triages" a week. Everyone agreed they should do another week of daily "Triages." Larry told me that he was surprised at the enthusiasm everyone showed about having daily "Triages" for another week but acknowledged that during the "Triage," gaps were identified more quickly with solutions and action items agreed upon right then. He said that he felt we were moving quickly through the project.

The following week, we moved to three "Triages" and then dropped to once a week for another two weeks to make sure processes were going smoothly. The "Pilot Program" resulted in new reporting that helped analyze the call patterns and other metrics, which led to improved operational decisions within the help desk organization. Everyone in this 650-seat virtual work at home environment had been trained on the new processes, the schedule in the help desk was more efficient, and the employees at the help desk had been retrained. Employees utilized the help desk without long wait times and were no longer frustrated. They also appreciated that management had addressed the issues.

As part of the communication strategy, I produced three videos per week in order to update everyone. This "Pilot Program" became the foundation for a new process that helped them drive to the top 15% of the over 30 international vendors that were also providing technical support for this Fortune 50 client.

Keys to a Successful "Triage"

The "Triage" tool takes practice. When people are working from home or in different locations, they may try to use the time for chitchatting and nonproductive conversations. Even in person, conference rooms can quickly become gathering places for socializing, instead of productivity. "Triages" are supposed to be quick. Participants can be anywhere and just dial in. In some of my organizations, we have a "War Room" bridge that we use for "Triages" when we are driving a product launch or a seasonal surge of activity.

When the "Triage" tool is used effectively, your teams will be able to move faster through a gap or project, saving time, money, and stress. As with all the tools in *The Leadership Toolbox*, there is no right or wrong way to utilize the tool. Be creative. Ask your participants what they want accomplished. If it isn't as productive as you need it to be, change the format. Remember, there are no "mistakes."

I have had "Triages" with 50 leaders on a conference bridge from multiple departments and locations and different levels of employees. I have also had "Triages" with a small handful of people. Sometimes "Triage" participants don't talk. They are only there to observe. Questions can be asked verbally or chatted to the person leading the meeting. You can also put the challenge(s) up on a discussion board. Someone can take notes and then email them to everyone. In some organizations, we post the discussion notes in a blog format on the communication board and then people can put their questions below the challenge for consideration at the next "Triage."

You can utilize "Triages" as part of your leadership development activities. Invite a few front-line employees that are showing promise to a supervisor "Triage" to get them exposed to something new, and then later, they can participate. You can invite a supervisor to a middle management "Triage," a middle-manager to a director-level "Triage," or a director to a VP-level "Triage" – all as part of your leadership development program.

In some organizations, we have set up a special text number to alert employees and leaders of a "Triage." Employees can set up a special ringtone on their phones to alert them to the text. This instills a sense of urgency. Employees are relieved that a challenge can be diffused quickly without derailing the organization. It motivates them, increasing employee engagement and job satisfaction.

This is one of the tools that I have successfully used thousands of times in my career. It's one of the tools that I credit for helping me lead all sizes of organizations across the finish line to a level of success they thought they never could achieve.

Final Thoughts

When I was 16 years old, my dad asked me a question that has stayed with me throughout my life. He asked, "Vicki, when your life is over, and they bury you six feet under, what will your legacy be? What will people say about you? What will you leave on this earth?" I had no answer for him at the time. In fact, at only 16 years old, I'd never even thought about it. Unfortunately, my Dad left this earth when I was 29 years old, but I believe in my heart that he knew I would leave an imprint on people's lives, because he raised me to do so.

Today, I would answer his question by saying, "Well, Dad, I have been asked by CEOs and senior-level executives to help them turn around and grow their organizations. These business leaders felt stuck and what they were doing just wasn't working. Their profits were eroding, or they were operating in the red. Their clients were threatening to fire them. Customers and employees weren't happy, and their companies were plagued with high employee absenteeism. They also couldn't retain their employees, which was costing them millions of dollars.

"I met these challenges head-on and, along the way, developed a set of tools that have helped dozens of businesses address their challenges while improving their companies. I approach every day with the goal of serving people and making a difference in their lives. I want them to feel better about themselves and grow, so they feel like they are contributing to others and the success of their companies. I want to help people exceed their clients' and customers' expectations when they come to work each day.

"When I leave this lifetime, Dad, I want to leave a legacy of helping companies and people achieve their goals. I want people to say that the tools in *The Leadership Toolbox* improved their lives and their businesses, helping them reach a higher level of success. In the end, Dad, I want to, in some small way, make a difference."

Why *The Leadership Toolbox* Works

The tools in *The Leadership Toolbox* have been taught to thousands of people in my career and have stood the test of time. They have been effectively utilized in numerous scenarios, with various organizational structures and industries, and with different types of people, including volunteers. People have consistently told me that the tools are easy to learn, quickly implemented, and always successful. As the business landscape has evolved throughout my career, with new concepts and initiatives emerging, the tools in *The Leadership Toolbox* have continuously proven themselves effective at moving corporations forward, even in regard to the latest industry trends.

I was having dinner with a senior vice president who oversees diversity and inclusion for a major media company. As we were talking, she seemed to have a surprising revelation and declared, "Your tools have been cultivating *authentic inclusion* inside companies your entire career!" While this was of no surprise to me, I did appreciate that she recognized how *The Leadership Toolbox* could add value to companies as they drove their corporate inclusion initiatives. The tools give the power back to the people to create and build a culture of authentic inclusion. They work because people from all different walks of life are creating and developing the ideas to move an organization forward. When the authentic inclusive culture inside your company mirrors your customer base, service and product offers are naturally enhanced.

The Leadership Toolbox also works because it drives employee engagement and retention, encouraging emotional buy-in to the results of your company. These tools can be enhanced when utilized as building blocks and cultivated in real time to immediately address real-live business challenges inside your organization. A leadership mindset is developed, so employees come to work every day thinking about how they can best serve customers, clients, and co-workers to help "Make Money," "Save Money," and "Mitigate Risk" inside your company. As more and more employees learn the tools in *The Leadership Toolbox*, they become habits and part of the fabric of your organization. When this happens, you can duplicate or multiply your efforts by the hundreds or thousands and successfully build that chain reaction of success that I have spoken about throughout this book.

As leaders, we have the power to move our organizations forward, but we need courage to make changes in ourselves. It takes determination to try new tools, perfect those tools, and cultivate new leadership habits that can withstand the challenges of everyday business, especially when people and business needs are pulling us from all different directions. Great leaders do what others won't do. Sometimes it takes sheer guts to look in "The Mirror" and ask ourselves the tough questions, especially when we are afraid of what those answers might be. Our fear can immobilize us and keep us from moving forward. But if we have the courage to try something we've never done before and trust that our employees will rise to the challenge, we can achieve our "Big Picture" – and our employees can be part of the celebration, because they were a valuable part of the solution.

Throughout my years of utilizing *The Leadership Toolbox*, I have realized that as leaders we end up spending our time in one of two ways: 1) on the front end by being proactive and utilizing the tools to make deliberate choices and taking deliberate actions or 2) on the back end, when we are in crisis mode or having business challenges that can erode the bottom line and emotionally drain our teams. I, for one, would rather be proactive and these tools help you do just that. They can become part of leadership development programs. When used as mentoring tools, they can build a strong leadership team and bench, where an organization can quickly move forward to drive employee engagement, satisfaction, and growth.

Today, I leave you *The Leadership Toolbox*. I leave these tools in your most capable hands. If you utilize them, I know you will build your own legacy and make a difference in your life, as well as the lives of others. The tools will help your company build a chain reaction of success that better serves your employees, clients, and customers, while gaining market share and increasing revenue and profitability.

I want to thank every company that I have worked with in my career for allowing me to utilize my tools and build great organizations that performed well. Thank you to the thousands of employees who helped me vet *The Leadership Toolbox*. You encouraged me to write this book and told me that these concepts are easy to understand and easy to use. It's been an honor and privilege to watch you grow as leaders and individuals. To my clients, thank you for letting me serve you and bring my tools to help your organizations achieve great results faster than you ever thought possible.

In closing, I want to thank you, the reader, for this opportunity to share my tools and my "Third-Party Stories" that span my career. As you utilize the tools in *The Leadership Toolbox*, please let me know about your success and share your own "Third-Party Stories." I will be cheering you on.

See you at the TOP!

Vicki

About the Author

Vicki Brackett has spent her entire career driving operational change and building leadership programs that engage and inspire both leaders and employees to achieve results that impact business in a big way. With a core belief that customer and client success directly relates to employee engagement, Vicki has developed leadership tools and strategies to engage employees and make process changes quickly, so business leaders don't have any surprises when looking at their key performance indicators or an organization's P&L.

For over 20 years, Vicki has helped turn around businesses that weren't generating profit or meeting customer service goals. These experiences gave her the opportunity to develop a unique leadership style that utilizes motivational and inspirational foundations to encourage employees and leadership to be pro-active, and tackle process improvements in real time, even when business is moving quickly. These changes impact the customer experiences, increasing the lifetime value of customer relationships and level of employee satisfaction.

Vicki's experience, which includes leading organizations from 50 to over 2,000 employees, has led her to understand that leaders will spend time on their organizations in one of two ways. They will either spend it on the front end to proactively engage employees, re-engineer processes, and mentor leadership, or they will spend it on the back end doing "damage control" to try and turn around less than acceptable or failing key performance indicators.

Employees and leaders alike value Vicki's optimistic attitude and belief that anything is possible, as she opens the door to employee-driven initiatives that routinely exceed organizational goals. Having led small, medium and Fortune 500 organizations through start up, turnaround, and rapid growth scenarios, she has a proven track record of increasing sales conversion and customer service satisfaction scores, along with repeat business and profits, while decreasing costs, employee absenteeism and employee attrition to save companies millions of dollars.

The tools and strategies in *The Leadership Toolbox* are the culmination of Vicki's decades of business experience. These tools were developed over her career and vetted by thousands of employees in dozens of organizations.

Today, Vicki speaks, trains, consults, and mentors corporate leaders, helping them to move key performance indicators in the right direction, all while increasing employee satisfaction. Her passionate, charismatic and optimistic personality is contagious and drives an enjoyable workplace, which she believes enhances the results even more.

To engage Vicki as a speaker for your upcoming event, or to get more information on leadership mentoring or consulting for your company, you can contact info@vickibrackett.com.

To engage Vicki as a speaker for your upcoming event, or to get more information on leadership mentoring or consulting for your company, you can contact info@vickibrackett.com.

For volume book discounts contact info@TheLeadershipToolbox.com.

Other Resources

https://www.VickiBrackett.com

https://www.TheLeadershipToolbox.com

 https://www.linkedin.com/in/vickibrackett/

 Vicki Brackett - Leadership & Operations Consultant
https://www.facebook.com/VickiBrackett.Consultant

 The Leadership Toolbox Facebook Page

 @vickibrackett

CPSIA information can be obtained
at www.ICGtesting.com
Printed in the USA
BVHW041257140319
542683BV00010B/104/P